Based on the *New York Times* bestseller *Ask and It Is Given* by

ESTHER AND JERRY HICKS

(The Teachings of Abraham™)

Ask and It Is Given

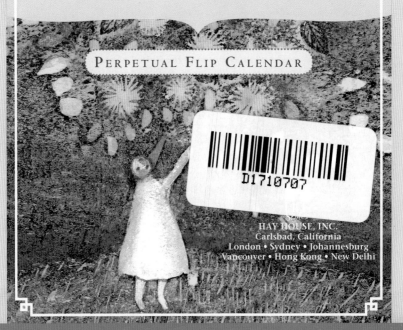

PERPETUAL FLIP CALENDAR

HAY HOUSE, INC.
Carlsbad, California
London • Sydney • Johannesburg
Vancouver • Hong Kong • New Delhi

A CALENDAR TO USE YEAR AFTER YEAR

We hope you enjoyed this Hay House Lifestyles calendar. If you would like to receive a free catalog featuring additional Hay House books and products, or if you would like information about the Hay Foundation, please contact:

Hay House, Inc., P.O. Box 5100, Carlsbad, CA 92018-5100

(760) 431-7695 or **(800) 654-5126**
(760) 431-6948 (fax) or **(800) 650-5115 (fax)**
www.hayhouse.com® • **www.hayfoundation.org**

• • • • • • • • • • • • • • • • • •

Published and distributed in Australia by:
Hay House Australia Pty. Ltd., 18/36 Ralph St., Alexandria NSW 2015
Phone: 612-9669-4299 • Fax: 612-9669-4144 • www.hayhouse.com.au

Published and distributed in the United Kingdom by:
Hay House UK, Ltd., 292B Kensal Rd., London W10 5BE • Phone: 44-20-8962-1230
Fax: 44-20-8962-1239 • www.hayhouse.co.uk

Published and distributed in the Republic of South Africa by:
Hay House SA (Pty), Ltd., P.O. Box 990, Witkoppen 2068
Phone/Fax: 27-11-706-6612 • orders@psdprom.co.za

Published in India by: Hay House Publishers India, Muskaan Complex,
Plot No. 3, B-2, Vasant Kunj, New Delhi 110 070 • Phone: 91-11-4176-1620
Fax: 91-11-4176-1630 • www.hayhouseindia.co.in

Distributed in Canada by: Raincoast , 9050 Shaughnessy St., Vancouver, B.C.
V6P 6E5 • Phone: (604) 323-7100 • Fax: (604) 323-2600 • www.raincoast.com

Editorial supervision: Jill Kramer
Design: Amy Gingery
Illustrations: Kristina Swarner

The material in this calendar is based on the book *Ask and It Is Given* by Esther and Jerry Hicks (Hay House, 2004)

ISBN: 978-1-4019-1053-2

Printed in China

Additional Calendars Available from Hay House

EVERYDAY WISDOM Perpetual Flip Calendar,
by Dr. Wayne W. Dyer

I CAN DO IT® Calendar, by Louise L. Hay

INSPIRATION Perpetual Flip Calendar,
by Dr. Wayne W. Dyer

MESSAGES FROM YOUR ANGELS Perpetual Flip Calendar,
by Doreen Virtue, Ph.D.

THE POWER OF INTENTION Perpetual Flip Calendar,
by Dr. Wayne W. Dyer

WISE WORDS Perpetual Flip Calendar—compiled from New
Dimensions® radio interviews by Michael Toms

A YEAR OF DAILY WISDOM Perpetual Flip Calendar,
by Marianne Williamson

All of the above are available at your local bookstore,
or may be ordered by visiting Hay House (see next page
for contact information).

Tune in to **HayHouseRadio.com®** for the best in
inspirational talk radio featuring top Hay House authors!
And, sign up via the Hay House USA Website to receive the Hay House
online newsletter and stay informed about what's going on with your
favorite authors. You'll receive bimonthly announcements about: Discounts
and Offers, Special Events, Product Highlights, Free Excerpts,
Giveaways, and more!
www.hayhouse.com®

Dear Friends,

Those who are not yet aware of the powerful Stream of Well-Being that flows to each of us from the Non-physical find the utilization of this *Ask and It is Given Calendar* irrationally powerful. When you do not understand the power behind it, it almost seems magical. However, it is not magic. It is the natural result of you tapping into the loving stream of Non-Physical Energy that has come forth onto these pages in response to the asking of millions of people.

We love this calendar, and feel so much appreciation for the way this focused Energy enhances our lives, and we are so happy that you now can begin to receive the benefit of its power.

Our love,
Esther & Jerry

ABOUT THE AUTHORS

Esther and **Jerry Hicks** produce and present the leading-edge Abraham-Hicks teachings on the art of allowing our natural Well-Being to come forth. While presenting open workshops in up to 60 cities a year, they've created more than 700 books, audios, CDs, and videos. Their internationally acclaimed Website is: **www.abraham-hicks.com**.

Also Available from Hay House by Esther and Jerry Hicks

The Amazing Power of Deliberate Intent (also available in Spanish)

Ask and It Is Given (also available in Spanish)

Ask and It Is Given Cards

The Astonishing Power of Emotions

The Law of Attraction

The Law of Attraction Cards (available February 2008)

Manifest Your Desires (available June 2008)

Sara, Book 1: The Foreverness of Friends of a Feather

Sara, Book 2: Solomon's Fine Featherless Friends

Sara, Book 3: A Talking Owl Is Worth a Thousand Words! (available April 2008)

The Teachings of Abraham Well-Being Cards

JANUARY 1

We are called
Abraham, and we are
speaking to you from the Non-
Physical dimension. In this Non-
Physical realm, we do not use words, for
we do not require language. We also do
not have tongues with which to speak or
ears with which to hear, although we do
communicate perfectly with one another.
Our Non-Physical language is one of
vibration, and our Non-Physical
communities, or families, are
those of intention.

DECEMBER 31

Be easy about all of
this. Life is supposed to be
fun, you know. It is our powerful desire that you return to your
state of self-appreciation. We want
you to feel love for your life, for
the people of your world, and,
most of all, for yourself.

JANUARY 2

Abraham is a
family of Non-Physical
Beings naturally assembled by
our powerful intention to remind
you, our physical extensions, of the
Laws of the Universe that govern all
things. It is our intention to help you
remember that you are extensions of
Source Energy; that you are blessed,
loved Beings; and that you have
come forth into this physical
time-space reality to
joyously create.

DECEMBER 30

Now that you
understand that your
intent is simply to reach a better-
feeling emotion, it is our expectation
that the *Moving-Up-the-Emotional-Scale
Process* will free you from troubling negative emotions that you have been experiencing for years. And as you gently and
gradually release the resistance you have
unknowingly gathered, you will begin
to experience improvements in your
life experiences . . . in all troubling areas of your life.

JANUARY 3

Words really do not
teach. Your true knowledge
comes from your own life experience. And while you will be a
constant gatherer of experience and
knowledge, your life is not only about
that—it is about fulfillment, satisfaction, and joy. Your life is about the
continuing expression of who
you truly are.

DECEMBER 29

Of course, it is always better when you achieve an improved state of emotion deliberately, but even when the improved emotions are discovered naturally and unconsciously, each movement up the scale of emotions now gives you access to something even more improved. Once you find the relief that *anger* and *blame* can offer from those suffocating emotions of *powerlessness* and *grief,* you can move even more quickly up what we call the *Vibrational Emotional Scale.*

We are communicating
with you at many levels of
your awareness, all at the same
time, but you will only receive
whatever you are now ready to
receive. Everyone will not get the
same thing from this material,
but every reading will net you
something more.

DECEMBER 28

Finding the perfect word to describe the way you feel is not essential to a *Moving-Up-the-Emotional-Scale Process,* but feeling the emotion is important—and finding ways to improve the feeling is even more important. In other words, this game is strictly about discovering thoughts that give you feelings of relief.

JANUARY 5

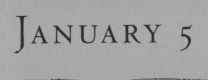

Do you know what you want? Are you enjoying the evolution of your desire? If you are among the rare humans who answered, "Yes, I'm enjoying the evolution of my desire," then you understand who you are and what this physical life experience is really all about.

DECEMBER 27

There is noth-
ing that you or anyone
else has ever wanted that exists
for any other reason than that you
think you will feel better in the achieving of it. Once you consciously identify
your current state of emotion, it becomes
easier for you to understand whether you
are choosing thoughts that move you closer
to your desired destination or farther from
your desired destination. If you make the
improved feeling or emotion your real
destination, then anything and
everything that you want will
quickly follow.

You said, "I will go forth into the physical time-space reality among other Beings, and I will assume an identity with a clear and specific perspective." You said, "I will love pouring myself into this physical body, into physical time-space reality, for that environment will cause me to focus the powerful Energy that is me into something more specific. And in the specifics of that focus, there will be powerful motion forward— and joy."

Here is a rule of thumb that will help you: *Make a decision about what you want, focus your attention there, and find the feeling-place of it—and you are there instantly. There is no reason for you to suffer or struggle your way to or through anything.*

JANUARY 7

There is nothing that you cannot be, do, or have; and we want to assist you in achieving that. But we love where you are right now, even if you do not, because we understand how joyful the journey to where you want to go will be.

If you believe
that something is good,
and you do it—it benefits
you. If you believe that something is bad, and you do it—it is
a very detrimental experience. Get
clear and happy about whichever
choice you make, because it is
your contradiction that causes
the majority of the contradiction in vibration.

JANUARY 8

You were born
with an innate knowledge
that you do create your own
reality. And, in fact, that knowledge is
so basic within you that when someone
attempts to thwart your own creation, you
feel an immediate discord within yourself.
Within you, today, lives the knowledge that
you *are* the creator of your own life experience; that absolute freedom exists as the
basis of your true experience; and that,
ultimately—the creation of your life
experience is absolutely and
only up to you.

DECEMBER 24

You are an Eternal Being always projecting from Non-Physical, and sometimes that projection is into a physical personality. When the physical personality is complete, for this time—then there is a withdrawal of focus.

JANUARY 9

These teachings of Abraham are written to assist you in consciously returning to the knowledge that you are free and that you always *have been* free—and that you always *will be* free to make your own choices. There is no satisfaction in allowing someone else to attempt to create your reality. In fact—it is not *possible* for anyone else to create your reality.

Every death is
brought about by the
culmination of the vibration
of the Being. There is not an
exception to that. No one, beast or
human, makes their transition into
the Non-Physical without it being
the vibrational consensus that is
within them—so every death is
a suicide because every death
is self-imposed.

You are an
Eternal Being who has
chosen to participate in this specific physical life experience for many
wonderful reasons. And this time-space
reality on planet Earth serves as a plat-
form in which you are able to focus your
perspective for the purpose of specific
creation. You are Eternal Consciousness,
currently in this wonderful physical
body for the thrill and exhilara-
tion of specific focus and
creation.

You could remain in
your body indefinitely if you
would allow your environment to
continue to produce new, continuing,
life-summoning, pure, unresisted desire.
You could be one who opened your vortex
to continually find new things to want, and
those desires would continue to summon the
Life Force through you. In other words, you
are living raucously, you are living joyously,
you are living rambunctiously, and you are
living passionately . . . *and then, from that
same framework, you make a conscious
decision to make your transition.*

These teachings
of Abraham are written
to help you understand that you
have the ability to always allow your
true nature to pour through you, and that
as you learn to *consciously* allow your full
connection with the You that is your Source,
your experience will be one of absolute joy.
By consciously choosing the direction of
your thoughts, you can be in constant
connection with Source Energy, with
God, with joy, and with all that
you consider to be good.

DECEMBER 21

Do you have to think
specific positive thoughts about
your body in order for it to be the
way you want it to be? No. But you
have to *not* think the specific negative thoughts. If you could never again
think about your body and, instead,
just think pleasant thoughts, your
body would reclaim its natural
place of wellness.

Well-Being is the basis of
All-That-Is. It flows to you and
through you. You have only to
allow it. Like the air you breathe,
you have only to open, relax,
and draw it into your Being.

Any disease could be healed in a matter of days—any disease—if distraction from it could occur and a different vibration dominate—and the healing time is about how much mix-up there is in all of that, for any malady in your physical body took a lot longer in coming than it takes to release it.

JANUARY 13

Your motion forward is
inevitable; it must be. You cannot
help but move forward. But you
are not here on a quest to move
forward—you are here to experience outrageous joy. That is
why you are here.

DECEMBER 19

Wellness that is
being allowed, or wellness
that is being denied, is all about
the mind-set, the mood, the attitude,
or the practiced thoughts. There is not
one exception in any human or beast,
because you can patch them up again and
again—but they will just find another way
of reverting to the natural rhythm of
their mind. *Treating the body really
is about treating the mind. It is all
psychosomatic—every bit of it.
No exceptions.*

JANUARY 14

"Why is it
taking me so long to
get what I want?" It is not
because you are not intelligent
enough or worthy enough. The
only reason you have not already
gotten what you desire is because
you are holding yourself in a
vibrational pattern that does
not match the vibration
of your desire.

DECEMBER 18

Do not let anyplace that you are standing frighten you. All it is, is a by-product of some Energy alignment that only gives you stronger clarity about what you want—and, most important— greater sensitivity about whether you are in a receiving mode or locked off from it.

Gently and gradually, piece by piece, release your resistant thoughts, which are the only disallowing factors involved. Your increasing relief will be the indicator that you are releasing resistance, just as your feelings of increased tension, anger, frustration, and so on have been your indicators that you have been adding to your resistance.

The question that often arises is: "Well, what about the little ones? What about the unhealthy babies?" And we say that they have been exposed to a vibration, even in the womb, which caused them to disallow the Well-Being that would have been there otherwise. But once they are born, no matter what their disability, if they could be encouraged to thoughts that would allow the Well-Being, then even after the body is fully formed, it could be regenerated into something that is well.

JANUARY 16

Well-Being is
lined up outside your
door. Everything you have
ever desired, whether spoken or
unspoken, has been transmitted by
you vibrationally. It has been heard
and understood by Source and has
been answered, and now you are
going to *feel* your way into allowing yourself to receive it, one
feeling at a time.

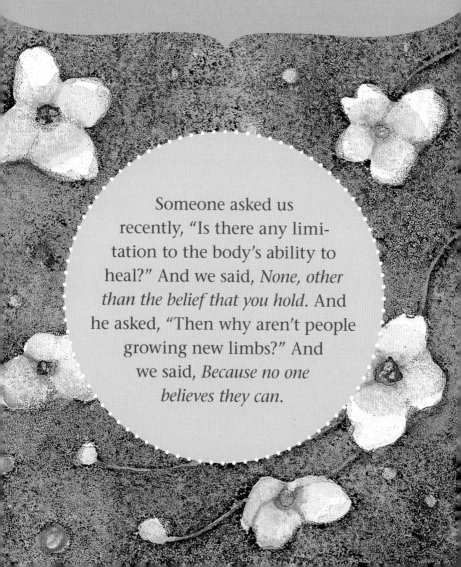

DECEMBER 16

Someone asked us recently, "Is there any limitation to the body's ability to heal?" And we said, *None, other than the belief that you hold*. And he asked, "Then why aren't people growing new limbs?" And we said, *Because no one believes they can*.

JANUARY 17

Everything in your physical environment was created from Non-Physical perspective by that which you call Source. And just as Source created you and your world—through the power of focused thought—you are continuing to create your world from your Leading-Edge place in this time-space reality.

DECEMBER 15

There is no
condition that you cannot
modify into something more,
any more than there is any paint-
ing that you cannot repaint. There are
many limiting thoughts in the human
environment that can make it seem that
these so-called incurable illnesses or
unchangeable conditions cannot be
changed—*but we say that they are
only "unchangeable" because
you believe they are.*

You and that which
you call Source are the same.
You cannot be separated from
Source. When we think of you,
we think of Source. When we think
of Source, we think of you. Source
never offers a thought that
causes separation from you.

DECEMBER 14

It is natural for
your body to be well. And
so, your goal is to be as comfortable as possible, and to breathe as
deeply as you can while still remaining
comfortable. There is nothing for you to do
other than to relax and breathe. You will very
likely begin to feel soft, gentle sensations in
your body. Smile, and acknowledge that this
is *Source Energy* specifically answering your
cellular request. You are now *feeling* the
healing process. Do nothing to try to
help it or intensify it. Just relax
and breathe—and allow it.

Source is always
fully available to you,
and Well-Being is constantly
extended to you; and often you
are in the state of *allowing* this
Well-Being, but sometimes you
are not. *We want to assist you
in <u>consciously</u> allowing your
connection, more of the
time, to Source.*

There is not
anything in all of the
Universe more delicious than
to have a desire that you are a
vibrational match to, and—in that
alignment of your being connected
to Source Energy—being inspired to
an action. That is the furthest extension of the *Creation Process*—there is
no action in all of the Universe
that is more delicious than
inspired action.

As extensions of Non-Physical Energy, you are taking thought beyond that which it has been before—and, through contrast, you will come to conclusions or decisions. And once you align with your desire, the Non-Physical Energy that creates worlds will flow through you . . . which means enthusiasm, passion, and triumph. That is your destiny.

DECEMBER 12

Setting goals is
like delegating to your
Universal Manager. And achieving the vibration of *allowing* is like
standing back and trusting your manager to set things into place, trusting that
when another decision is needed from
you, you will be aware of it. You are not *delegating* your life—you are *creating* your life.
You are becoming the visionary, in the
creation mode, but there will still be
plenty of things that you will want
to *do*. We in no way want to steer
you away from action.
Action is fun.

JANUARY 21

From the Non-Physical, you created you; and now from the physical, you continue to create. We all must have objects of attention and desires that are ringing our bells in order to feel the fullness of who we are flowing through us for the continuation of All-That-Is. That desire is what puts the eternalness in eternity.

You may be saying to yourself, right now, "I'd love to have a manager—someone I can count on, someone who would work on my behalf." And we say to you, *You do have a manager who is that and much more. You have a "manager" who works continually on your behalf called the <u>Law of Attraction</u>—you have only to <u>ask</u> in order for your Universal Manager to jump to your request.*

JANUARY 22

Do not
underestimate the value
of your preferences, for the
evolution of your planet depends
upon those of you on the Leading
Edge of thought continuing to
fine-tune your desires. And the
contrast, or variety, provides the
perfect environment for the
formation of your per-
sonal preferences.

DECEMBER 10

Life is supposed to be
fun—it is supposed to feel
good! You are powerful creators,
and you are right on schedule. . . .
Savor more; fix less. Laugh more; cry
less. Anticipate positively more; anticipate negatively less. . . . . Nothing is
more important than that you feel
good—just practice that and
watch what happens.

As you are standing in the midst of contrast, new desires are radiating constantly from you in the form of vibrational signals that are received and answered by Source—and, in that moment, the Universe is expanding. . . . These teachings are not about the expanding Universe, or about Source answering your every request, or about your worthiness—for all of that is a given. They are about you putting yourself in a vibrational place of receiving all that you are asking for.

DECEMBER 9

Every resource you will ever
want or need is at your fingertips. All you have to do is identify
what you want to do with it, and
then practice the feeling-place
of what it will be like when
that happens.

You *do* create your own reality. No one else does. And you create your own reality even if you do not understand that you do so. For that reason, you often create by default. *When you are consciously aware of your own thoughts and are deliberately offering them, then you are the <u>deliberate</u> creator of your own reality—* and that is what you intended when you made the decision to come forth into this body.

December 8

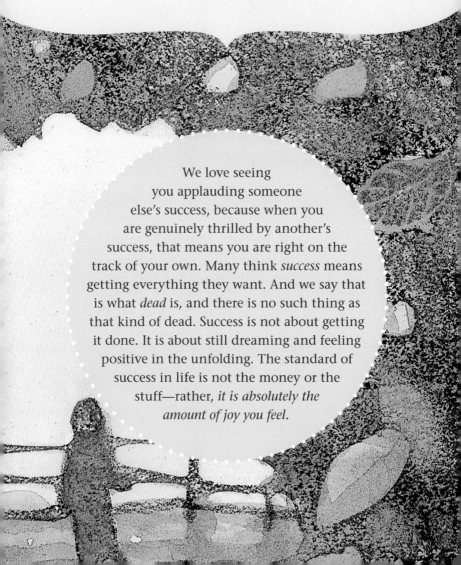

We love seeing
you applauding someone
else's success, because when you
are genuinely thrilled by another's
success, that means you are right on the
track of your own. Many think *success* means
getting everything they want. And we say that
is what *dead* is, and there is no such thing as
that kind of dead. Success is not about getting
it done. It is about still dreaming and feeling
positive in the unfolding. The standard of
success in life is not the money or the
stuff—rather, *it is absolutely the
amount of joy you feel.*

Your desires and beliefs
are just thoughts: "Ask and it
is given." You ask through your
attention, through your wanting,
through your desire—that is the
asking. Whether you desire it *to*
happen or you desire it *not* to
happen, you are asking.

DECEMBER 7

Feel
appreciation for
those who provide examples
of financial Well-Being. How
would you know prosperity was possible if there was not evidence of it around
you? It is all part of the contrast. Money is
not the root of happiness, but it is not the
"root of evil," either. Money is the result of
how somebody lines up Energy. If you do not
want money, do not attract it, but your criticism of others who have money holds you
in a place where things you *do* want,
such as wellness, clarity, and
Well-Being, cannot come
to you, either.

You
do not have to
use your words. You just
have to feel it in your Being:
*I desire this. I adore this. I appreciate
this,* and so on. That desire is the beginning of all attraction. . . . You never grow
tired of expansion or of creation, for there
is no ending to the new ideas of desires that
flow. With every new idea of something you
would like to experience, possess, or know
. . . will come its actualization or manifestation—and with that manifestation will also come a new perspective from which you
will desire.

DECEMBER 6

Your financial
decline will not elevate
the impoverished. . . . You
cannot get poor enough to help
the impoverished people thrive.
It is only in your thriving that you
have anything to offer anyone.
If you want to be of help to
others, be as tapped in, tuned
in, and turned on as you
can possibly be.

The contrast, or variety, never ends, so the sprouting forth of new desires will never end; and as that "asking" never ends, the "answering" never ceases to flow. And so, new contrasts, and new inspiring desires and perspectives, will be laid out eternally before you.

Spiritual versus material is not
the choice. Everything about this
manifestational experience is
Spiritual. It is all the end product of
Spirit. You have nothing to prove.
Be the Spiritual You and create
like a physical fiend.

You will never
cease to be; new desires
will be constantly born within you; Source will never stop
answering your desires; and your
expansion is, therefore, eternal. And
so, you may begin to relax if, in
this moment, there is something
that you desire that has not
yet come to fruition.

DECEMBER 4

There is no
"high work" or "low
work." There are just opportunities to focus. You can feel as
fulfilled and satisfied in any one task
as in any other, for you are on the
Leading Edge of thought, and Source is
flowing through you no matter what
your endeavor is. You can be joyful
in any endeavor where you
decide to allow the
Energy to flow.

JANUARY 29

It is our desire
that you become one who
is happy with that which you
are and with that which you have—
while at the same time being eager
for more. That is the optimal creative
vantage point: To stand on the brink of
what is coming, feeling eager, optimistic
anticipation—with no feeling of impa-
tience, doubt, or unworthiness hindering the receiving of it—that is
the *Science of Deliberate
Creation* at its best.

DECEMBER 3

Your role is
to utilize Energy. That
is why you exist. You are an
Energy-flowing Being—a focuser, a
perceiver. You are a creator, and there
is nothing worse in all of the Universe
than to come forth into the environment of great contrast, where desire is
easily born, and not allow Energy
to flow to your desire—that is a
true squandering of life.

There is a current that runs through everything. It exists throughout the Universe, and it exists throughout All-That-Is. It is the basis of the Universe, and as you begin to understand this basis of your world and begin to *feel for* your awareness of this Source Energy that is the basis of all things, you will then more clearly understand everything about your own experience and the experiences of those around you.

DECEMBER 2

So, what about
creating a very positive
current of financial abundance?
What about getting so good at visualizing that the money flows through
you easily? What about spending money,
and giving more people opportunity?
What better way could anyone spend
money than by putting it back into the
economy that gives more people work?
The more money you spend, the
more people benefit, and the more
people get in on the game and
dovetail with you.

Like learning to understand the basics of mathematics and then having the successful experience of understanding the results of their applications, once you have a formula for understanding your world that is always consistent, it will yield consistent results to you.

DECEMBER 1

There is nothing you cannot be, do, or have; you are blessed Beings, and you have come forth into this physical environment to create. There is nothing holding you back other than your own contradictory thoughts— and your emotion tells you whenever you have such thoughts.

You are, even in your physical expression of flesh, blood, and bone, a "Vibrational Being"; and everything you experience in your physical environment is vibrational. And, it is only through your ability to translate vibration that you are able to understand your physical world at all.

NOVEMBER 30

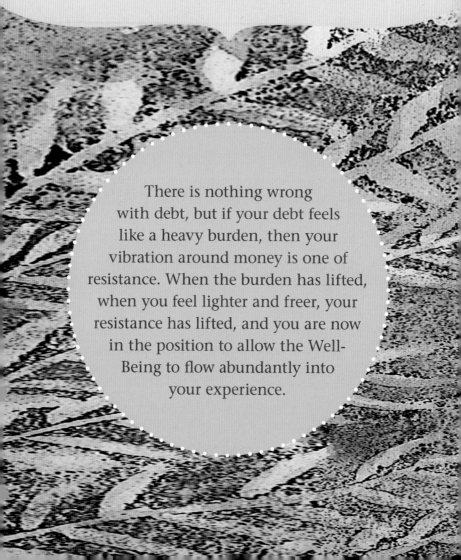

There is nothing wrong
with debt, but if your debt feels
like a heavy burden, then your
vibration around money is one of
resistance. When the burden has lifted,
when you feel lighter and freer, your
resistance has lifted, and you are now
in the position to allow the Well-
Being to flow abundantly into
your experience.

Your eyes, your ears . . . even your nose, tongue, and fingertips are translating vibrations . . . but your most sophisticated of vibrational interpreters by far are your emotions. By paying attention to the signals of your emotions, you can understand, with absolute precision, everything you are now living or have ever lived.

The more often
you play the *Finding the
Feeling-Place Process,* the better
you will be at playing it, and the
more fun it will become. When you
pretend, or selectively remember, you
activate new vibrations—and your point
of attraction shifts. And when your
point of attraction shifts, your life will
improve regarding every subject
for which you have found a
new *feeling-place.*

By paying atten-
tion to the way you feel,
you can fulfill your reason for
being here, and you can continue
your intended expansion in the joyful
way that you intended. By understanding your emotional connection to who-
you-really-are, you will come to understand not only what is happening in
your own world and why, but you
will also understand every other
living Being with whom
you interact.

Your intent, in
the *Finding the Feeling-
Place Process,* is to conjure images that cause you to offer a vibration that *allows* money. Your goal is
to create images that *feel* good to you.
Your goal is to find the *feeling-place* of
what it would be like to have enough
money rather than finding the
feeling-place of what it is like to
not have enough money.

FEBRUARY 4

Every thought vibrates, every thought radiates a signal, and every thought attracts a matching signal back. We call that process the *Law of Attraction*. The *Law of Attraction* says: *That which is like unto itself is drawn.*

The Universe does not
know if you are offering your
vibration because you are *living*
what you are living, or because
you are *imagining* that you are
living it. In either case, it answers
the vibration—and the manifestation must follow.

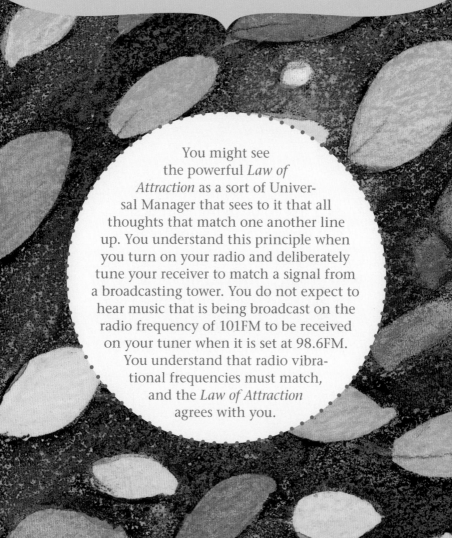

You might see the powerful *Law of Attraction* as a sort of Universal Manager that sees to it that all thoughts that match one another line up. You understand this principle when you turn on your radio and deliberately tune your receiver to match a signal from a broadcasting tower. You do not expect to hear music that is being broadcast on the radio frequency of 101FM to be received on your tuner when it is set at 98.6FM. You understand that radio vibrational frequencies must match, and the *Law of Attraction* agrees with you.

As you focus upon what it *feels* like to be living your desire, you cannot, at the same time, be *feeling the absence* of your desire, so with practice, you can tip the scale, so to speak, so that even though your desire has not yet actually manifested, you are offering a vibration as if it has—and then it *must*.

Whatever you are giving
your attention to causes you to
emit a vibrational frequency, and
the vibrations that you offer equal
your asking, which equals your
point of attraction.

There is no value
in using happy-sounding
words if you do not *feel* happy.
The *Law of Attraction* is not responding to your words, but instead,
is responding to the vibrations that are
radiating from you. It is quite possible for
you to use all the right-sounding words at
the same time that you are in a state of
powerful resistance to your own Well-
Being, for the words you use are
not important—how you *feel*
is what matters.

If there is some-
thing you desire that you
currently do not have, you need
only put your attention upon it, and,
by the *Law of Attraction*, it will come to
you. However, if there is something that
you desire that you currently do *not* have,
and you put your attention upon your current state of *not-having-it*, then the *Law of
Attraction* will continue to match that
not-having-it vibration, so you will
continue to *not have that which
you desire*. It is *Law*.

Whatever your focus of attention, it is summoning the Life Force—and it is the feel of the Life Force that life is about. The reason that you are summoning it is inconsequential. In other words, it is every bit as possible to feel as much joy in the preparation of your taxes as in the planning of an ocean cruise.

FEBRUARY 8

When your
thoughts are a vibrational
match to your desire, you feel
good—your emotional range would
be from contentment to expectation to
eagerness to joy. But if you are giving your
attention to the lack, or absence, of your
desire, your emotions would range from feelings of pessimism to worry to discouragement
to anger to insecurity to depression. Your
emotions provide a wonderful *Guidance
System* for you, and if you pay attention
to them you will be able to guide
yourself to anything
you desire.

NOVEMBER 23

Your point of power is in the present because even though you may be thinking about the *past,* or you may be thinking about the *now,* or you may be thinking about the *future, you are doing it all right now.* You are vibrating *now.* The pulse is *now.* The vibrational offering is *now.* Any creative tension between the summoning of the Life Force and allowing it to flow through (the summoning and the allowing)—is all happening right here in the *now.*

By the powerful *Universal
Law of Attraction,* you draw to
yourself the essence of whatever you
are predominantly thinking about.
So if you are predominantly thinking
about the things that you desire, your life
experience reflects those things. And,
in the same way, if you are predominantly thinking about what you do
not want, your life experience
reflects those things.

NOVEMBER 22

The *Law of Attraction* is
so very powerful that when
you hold a thought for as little
as 17 seconds, another thought
like it will join it; and as those two
thoughts come together, there is
a combustion that occurs that
makes your thoughts even
more powerful.

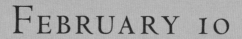

FEBRUARY 10

Whatever you are thinking
about is like planning a future
event. When you are appreciating,
you are planning. When you are
worrying, you are planning.
(Worrying is using your imagination to create something you
do not want.)

Sometimes some-
one will say to us, "But
Abraham, I cannot ignore this,
for it's true!" And we say, *It is only true
because someone has made it true by giving
their attention to it.* You see, what you are
actually saying here is, "Because someone
else has given attention to this and, therefore, by the *Law of Attraction,* invited it into
their own experience, I think I'll do the
same. In other words, even though I
don't want it, I'm obliged to create
it in my own reality because
someone else did."

Every thought,
every idea, every Being,
every thing, is vibrational, so
when you focus your attention on
something, even for a short period of
time, the vibration of your Being begins
to reflect the vibration of whatever you are
giving your attention to. The more you think
about it, the more you vibrate like it; the more
you vibrate like it, the more of that which
is like it is attracted to you. That trend in
attraction will continue to increase until
a different vibration is offered—and
then things that match *that*
vibration are drawn to
you, by you.

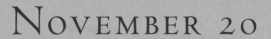

NOVEMBER 20

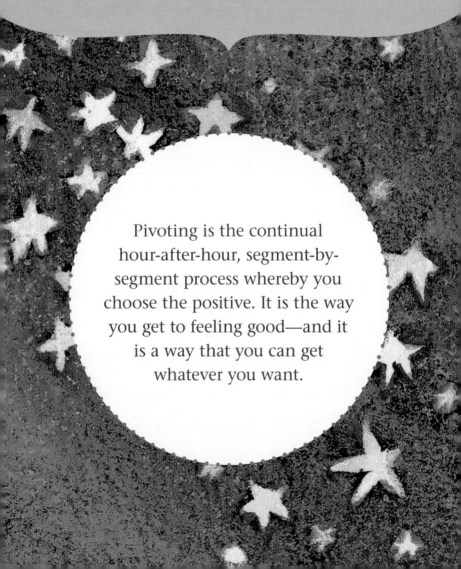

Pivoting is the continual
hour-after-hour, segment-by-
segment process whereby you
choose the positive. It is the way
you get to feeling good—and it
is a way that you can get
whatever you want.

When you understand the *Law of Attraction,* you are never surprised by anything that occurs in your experience, for you understand that you have invited every bit of it in—through your own thought process. *Nothing can occur in your life experience without your invitation of it through your thought.*

NOVEMBER 19

Do not try to save the
world; save yourself. That
means that you need to focus on
what makes you feel good. The *Process
of Pivoting* is the tool that will bring
you to what you *want*. It is the process
whereby you consciously decide: *Yes,
I want to look for what I want, and I
will no longer look in the direction
of the lack of what I want.*

There is
a very big vibra-
tional difference in your
thoughts of *appreciation* of your
mate, and in your thoughts of what
you would like to be *different* about
your mate. And your relationship with
your mate, without exception, reflects
the preponderance of your thoughts.
For, while you may not have done
it consciously, you have literally
thought your relationship
into being.

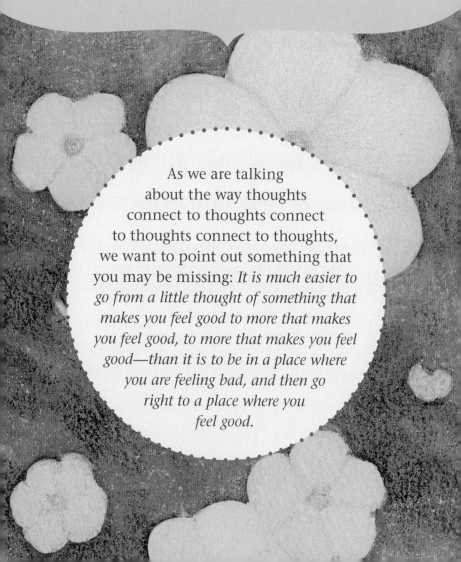

As we are talking
about the way thoughts
connect to thoughts connect
to thoughts connect to thoughts,
we want to point out something that
you may be missing: *It is much easier to
go from a little thought of something that
makes you feel good to more that makes
you feel good, to more that makes you feel
good—than it is to be in a place where
you are feeling bad, and then go
right to a place where you
feel good.*

FEBRUARY 14

Your desire for an improved financial condition cannot come to you if you often feel jealous of your neighbor's good fortune, for the vibration of your desire and the vibration of your jealous feelings are different vibrations. An understanding of your vibrational nature will make it possible for you to easily and deliberately create your own reality. And then, in time and with practice, you will discover that all desires that you hold can be easily realized—for there is nothing that you cannot be, do, or have.

NOVEMBER 17

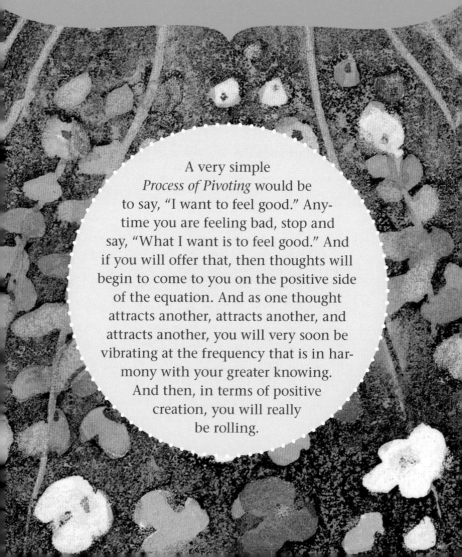

A very simple
Process of Pivoting would be
to say, "I want to feel good." Anytime you are feeling bad, stop and
say, "What I want is to feel good." And
if you will offer that, then thoughts will
begin to come to you on the positive side
of the equation. And as one thought
attracts another, attracts another, and
attracts another, you will very soon be
vibrating at the frequency that is in harmony with your greater knowing.
And then, in terms of positive
creation, you will really
be rolling.

FEBRUARY 15

You are Consciousness. You are Energy. You are Vibration. You are Electricity. You are Source Energy. You are Creator. You are on the Leading Edge of thought, and *even though it may seem odd to you at first, it will be helpful for you to begin to accept yourself as a Vibrational Being, for this is a Vibrational Universe in which you are living, and the Laws that govern this Universe are Vibrationally based.*

NOVEMBER 16

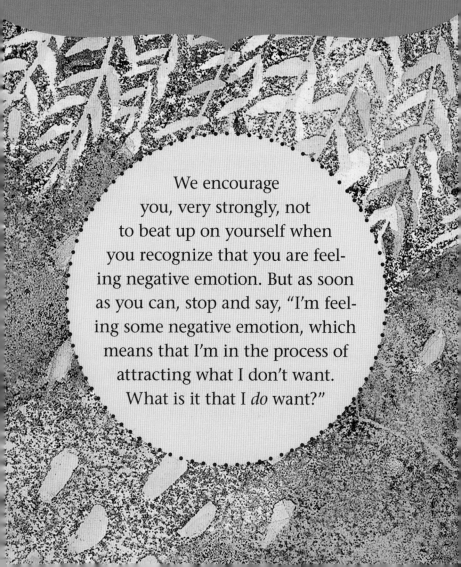

We encourage
you, very strongly, not
to beat up on yourself when
you recognize that you are feeling negative emotion. But as soon
as you can, stop and say, "I'm feeling some negative emotion, which
means that I'm in the process of
attracting what I don't want.
What is it that I *do* want?"

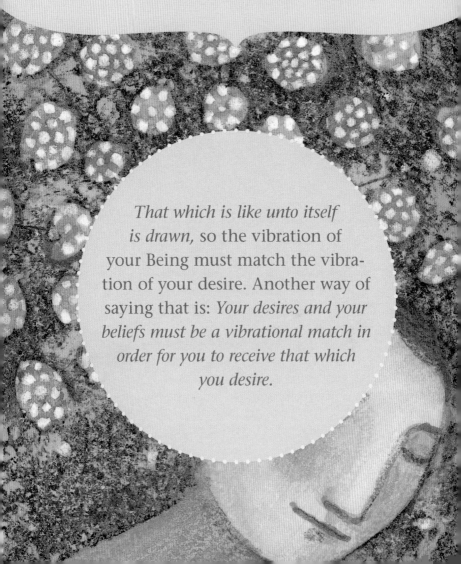

That which is like unto itself is drawn, so the vibration of your Being must match the vibration of your desire. Another way of saying that is: *Your desires and your beliefs must be a vibrational match in order for you to receive that which you desire.*

When you feel bad, you are in the process of attracting something that will not please you, and it is always because you are focused upon the lack of something you want. The *Process of Pivoting* is the conscious decision to identify what you *do* want. We do not want to imply that the feeling of negative emotion is a bad thing, because, very often, in the feeling of negative emotion, you are alerted to the fact that you are in the process of negatively attracting. And so, it is like a "warning bell." It is part of your *Emotional Guidance System.*

No matter what has caused your unique point of view to come about—it *has* come about. You do exist; you are thinking; you are perceiving; you are asking—and you are being answered. And All-That-Is is benefiting from your existence and from your point of view.

NOVEMBER 14

Never are you
more clear about what you
do want than when experiencing
what you do not want. And so, if you
will stop and say, "Something is important here, otherwise I would not be feeling
this negative emotion; I need to focus on what
I want," and then turn your attention to what
you *do* want—in that moment of turning your
attention, the negative emotion and the negative attraction will stop—and the positive
attraction will begin—and your feelings
will change from not feeling good
to feeling good. *That is the
<u>Process of Pivoting.</u>*

We call this discipline the *Art of Allowing*. It is the *Art of Allowing* the Well-Being—which makes up every particle of that which you are and that which you come from—to continue to flow through you as you continue to be.

As you are understanding that a feeling of negative energy is an indicator that you are not in harmony with your greater knowing, many of you have reached the point of saying, "I want to feel good more of the time." And we say that is a magnificent acknowledgment, because when you are saying, "I want to feel good," what you are really saying is: "I want to be in the place of positive attraction," or "I want to be in a place where the thoughts that I'm thinking as I'm feeling good are in harmony with my greater awareness."

Just as all of
your experience, from
the time of your birth into
your physical body until now,
has culminated into who *you* now
are, *all that has ever been experienced
by All-That-Is has culminated into
all that is now being experienced in
the physical life experience on
planet Earth.*

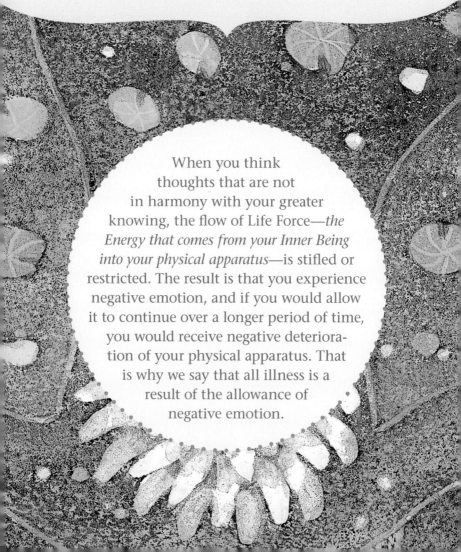

NOVEMBER 12

When you think
thoughts that are not
in harmony with your greater
knowing, the flow of Life Force—*the
Energy that comes from your Inner Being
into your physical apparatus*—is stifled or
restricted. The result is that you experience
negative emotion, and if you would allow
it to continue over a longer period of time,
you would receive negative deteriora-
tion of your physical apparatus. That
is why we say that all illness is a
result of the allowance of
negative emotion.

FEBRUARY 20

If your involve-
ment in your time-space
reality inspires within you any
sincere desire, then the Universe has
the means to supply the results that you
seek. . . . The Stream of Well-Being flows
even if you do not understand that it does;
but when you *consciously* become aligned
with it, your creative endeavors become
so much more satisfying—for then you
discover that there is absolutely
nothing that you desire that
you cannot achieve.

The
most important
thing to remember is
that you are the attractor of
your experience, and that you are
attracting it by virtue of the thoughts
that you are offering. Thoughts are
magnetic, and as you think a thought,
it will attract another and another and
another, until eventually you will
have a physical manifestation of
the vibrational essence of whatever has been the subject
of your thoughts.

It is not neces-
sary that you fully understand the complexities of this
eternally expanding environment in
order to reap the benefits of that which
it has become, but it *is* necessary that you
find a way to go with the flow of the Well-
Being that is stretched out before you. So,
in that effort, we offer these words: *There
is only a Stream of Well-Being that
flows. You can allow it or resist it,
but it flows just the same.*

See the *Process of Pivoting* as a gradual shifting of your point of attraction, and enjoy the positive results that must follow. It is not possible for you to consistently give your attention to what you *do* want and not receive it—for the *Law of Attraction* guarantees that whatever you are predominantly focused upon will flow into your experience.

You would not
enter a brightly lit room
and look for the "dark switch."
You would not expect to find a
switch that would flood an inky darkness into the room to cover the brightness
of the light—you would find a switch that
would resist the light, for in the absence of
light there is darkness. And, in like manner,
there is not a Source of "evil," but there
could be a resisting of that which you
believe is Good, just as there is not a
Source of sickness, but there could
be a resisting of the natural
Well-Being.

NOVEMBER 9

It is possible to
be focused in vibrational
opposition to what you really
desire without knowing you are.
It is like the opposite ends of a stick.
When you pick up a stick, you pick up
both ends. The *Pivoting Process* will help
you be more aware of which end of your
stick you are currently activating: the
end that is about what you want,
or the end that is about the
absence of what you want.

FEBRUARY 23

Without the
asking that precedes it,
there could be no answering. The
people of your times are benefiting
dramatically from the experiences of
those generations that preceded you, for
through the experiences that they lived, and
the desires that were generated within them,
the summoning began. And today, you are
the ones on the Leading Edge of reaping
the benefits of what those past generations asked for; at the same time, *you*
are continuing to ask, and *you*
are now summoning . . .
and on it goes.

NOVEMBER 8

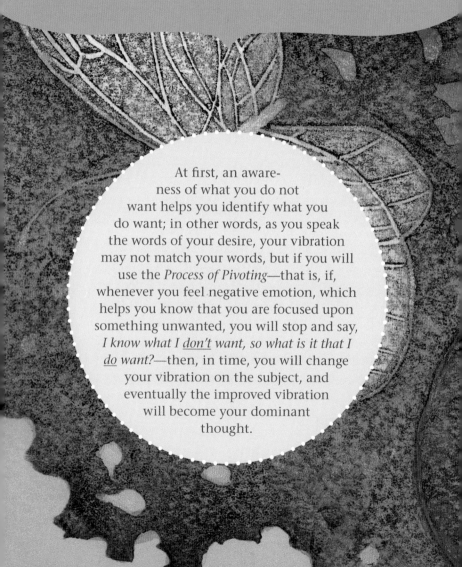

At first, an awareness of what you do not want helps you identify what you do want; in other words, as you speak the words of your desire, your vibration may not match your words, but if you will use the *Process of Pivoting*—that is, if, whenever you feel negative emotion, which helps you know that you are focused upon something unwanted, you will stop and say, *I know what I <u>don't</u> want, so what is it that I <u>do</u> want?*—then, in time, you will change your vibration on the subject, and eventually the improved vibration will become your dominant thought.

FEBRUARY 24

There are some
people experiencing intense
hardships or traumas; and because
of how they are living right now, their
asking is in a heightened and intense place.
And because of the intensity of their requests,
Source is responding in kind. And although
the person who is doing the asking is usually
so involved in the trauma that they are not
personally receiving the benefit of their own
asking, future generations—or even current generations who are not, right
now, disallowing—are receiving
the benefit of that *asking.*

NOVEMBER 7

You have to feel good about great
abundance before you will allow
the pleasure of great abundance to
flow into your experience.

We are giving
this to you by way of
helping you understand:
*There is an unlimited Stream of
Well-Being and an abundance of all
manner of things available to you at all
times—but you must be in alignment
with the receiving of those things.
You cannot stand in resistance
of them and receive them at
the same time.*

Seemingly magical
things will begin to occur as
soon as you achieve that wonderful feeling of financial abundance: The money you are currently
earning will seem to go further.
Unexpected amounts of money in
various increments will begin to
show up in your experience.

FEBRUARY 26

See yourself,
right where you are
now, as the beneficiary of the
powerful Stream of Well-Being.
Try to imagine that you are basking
in the flow of this powerful Stream.
Make an effort to feel yourself as
the Leading-Edge beneficiary of
this unlimited stream, and
smile and try to accept that
you are worthy of it.

An advantage of using the *Wallet Process* is that by holding a $100 bill and not spending it right away, you receive the vibrational advantage of it every time you even *think* about spending it. In other words, if you were to remember the hundred dollars in your wallet or your purse and spend it on the first thing that you noticed, you would receive the benefit of really *feeling* your financial well-being only once. But if you *mentally* spent that hundred dollars 20 or 30 times in that day, you will have received the vibrational *feeling* advantage of having spent two or three thousand dollars.

FEBRUARY 27

You (and how you
feel) are all that is respon-
sible for whether you let in your
inheritance of Well-Being or not. And
while those around you may influence
you, more or less, to allow or not allow that
Stream, it is ultimately all up to you. You can
open the floodgates and let in your Well-
Being, or you can choose thoughts that keep
you pinched off from what is yours—but
whether you allow it or resist it, the Stream
is constantly flowing to you, never ending, never tiring, and always there
for your reconsideration.

NOVEMBER 4

You do not have to actually
be abundant in order to *attract*
abundance, but you do have to *feel*
abundant—*any feeling of lack of
abundance causes a resistance that
does not allow abundance.*

Nothing has to change
in your environment or in the
circumstances that surround you
for you to begin to deliberately
allow your own connection to
the Stream of Well-Being. . . .
You are in the perfect place,
right now, to begin.

NOVEMBER 3

*Discard everything
from your experience that
is not essential to your <u>now.</u>* If you
could release those things you are not
wearing; release those things you are not
using, release them and leave your experience in a clearer place—then the things that
are more in harmony with who you are *now*
will more easily flow into your experience. *You
all have a capacity for attraction, and when your
process is clogged with stuff that you no longer
want, the new attraction is slower—and
then you end up with a feeling of
frustration or overwhelment.*

FEBRUARY 29
(FOR LEAP YEARS)

In every moment, you
are broadcasting a very specific
vibrational signal that is instantly
being understood and answered. And,
immediately, your present and future
circumstances begin changing in
response to the signal you are projecting. The entire Universe, right now,
is being affected by what you
are offering.

Sometimes people will tell us that they are not bothered by clutter, so we tell them that the *Clearing Clutter Process* is, then, unnecessary for them. However, since every piece of everything does carry a vibration, almost everyone really does feel better in an uncluttered environment.

MARCH 1

Your world, present and future, is directly and specifically affected by the signal that you are now transmitting. The personality that is You is really an Eternal personality, but who you are right now, and what you are thinking right now, is causing a focusing of Energy that is very powerful. This Energy that you are focusing is the same Energy that creates worlds. And it is, in this very moment, creating your world.

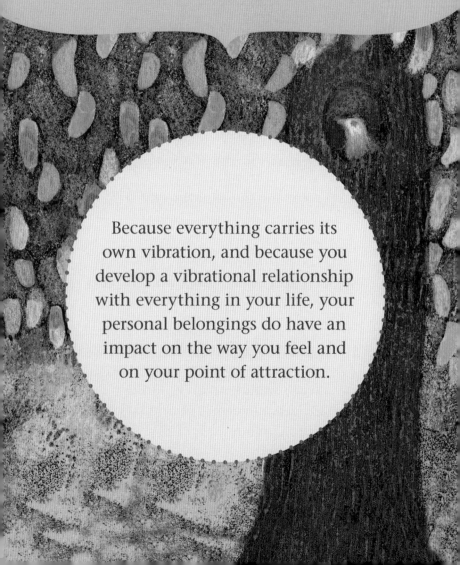

Because everything carries its own vibration, and because you develop a vibrational relationship with everything in your life, your personal belongings do have an impact on the way you feel and on your point of attraction.

Your feelings are the representatives of your Guidance System. In other words, the way you feel is your true indicator of your alignment with your Source, and of your alignment with your own intentions—both pre-birth and currently.

*Which thought feels
better?* To go into debt or to
wait until later? *To wait until later.
Which thought feels better?* To say that
you have settled for less, or to say that this
is part of your future experience? *To say that
this is part of my future experience.
Which thought feels better?*

Which feels better, to appreciate or to condemn?
Which feels better, to applaud what you have
done, or to feel critical that you did
not do enough?

Think about it: *Which
thought feels better?*

MARCH 3

Every thought
that has ever been thought
still exists, and whenever you
focus upon a thought, you activate
the vibration of that thought within
you. So, whatever you are currently giving
your attention to is an activated thought.
But when you turn your attention away from
a thought, it becomes dormant, or no longer
active. As you give more and more attention
to any thought, and as you focus upon it
and therefore practice the vibration of it,
the thought becomes an even bigger
part of your vibration—and you
could now call this practiced
thought a *belief.*

Your thoughts change the behavior of everyone and everything who has anything to do with you. For your thoughts absolutely equal your point of attraction, and the better you feel, the more everything and everyone around you improves. In the moment that you find an improved feeling, conditions and circumstances change to match your feeling. . . . Playing the *Which Thought Feels Better?* game will help you begin to realize the power that your own thoughts have to influence everything around you.

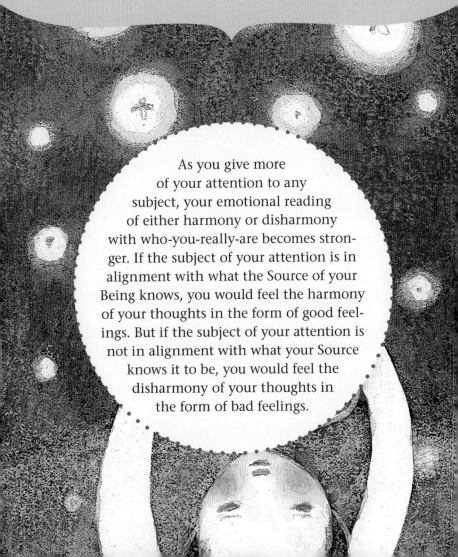

As you give more
of your attention to any
subject, your emotional reading
of either harmony or disharmony
with who-you-really-are becomes stronger. If the subject of your attention is in
alignment with what the Source of your
Being knows, you would feel the harmony
of your thoughts in the form of good feelings. But if the subject of your attention is
not in alignment with what your Source
knows it to be, you would feel the
disharmony of your thoughts in
the form of bad feelings.

Often, when you are interacting with others, you may be confused about whether the thought actually feels better to *you*, or whether you are offering it because you think it is the choice someone else would want you to make. *It is important to leave everyone else's ideas, desires, opinions, and beliefs aside while you identify, for yourself, how you feel.*

Every thought
that you give your atten-
tion to expands and becomes
a bigger part of your vibrational
mix. Whether it is a thought of
something you want or a thought
of something you do not want,
your attention to it invites the
essence of the thought into
your experience.

OCTOBER 28

Every subject is
really two subjects: something that you desire, and the
absence of something that you
desire. If you do not understand that
these are very different vibrational
frequencies, then you may believe that
you are focused on something that
you desire, when you may, in
fact, be focused in the
opposite direction.

Those who are
mostly observers thrive
in good times but suffer in bad
times because what they are observing is already vibrating, and as they
observe it, they include it in their vibrational countenance; and as they include
it, the Universe accepts that as their point
of attraction—and gives them more of
the essence of it. So, for an observer,
the better it gets, the better it gets; or
the worse it gets, the worse it gets.
However, one who is a visionary thrives in *all* times.

Whatever the subject of your desire, there is an orchestration that is being taken care of in response to the *Wouldn't It Be Nice If . . . ?* game that you are playing. So whenever you play this game and you trust that everything else will come into alignment—it will.

With your practiced attention to any subject, the *Law of Attraction* delivers circumstances, conditions, experiences, other people, and all manner of things that match your habitual dominant vibration. And as things begin to manifest around you that match the thoughts you have been holding, you now develop stronger and stronger vibrational habits or proclivities. And so, your once-small and insignificant thought has now evolved into a powerful belief—and your powerful beliefs will always be played out in your experience.

When you say,
"Wouldn't it be nice if this
desire would come to me?" you
achieve an expectation that is much
less resistant in nature. Your question to
yourself naturally elicits from you a more
positive, expectant response. And so, this
simple but powerful game will cause a raising
of your vibration and an improvement in your
point of attraction because it naturally orients
you toward the things that you want. The
Wouldn't It Be Nice If . . . ? Process will
help you let in the things that you
have been asking for, on
all subjects.

MARCH 8

Your sense of
taste or smell or hearing
or sight is not usually the way
you recognize a hot stove, but as you
approach the stove with your body, the
sensors in your skin let you know if the
stove is hot. And in the same way that you
utilize your sensitive, sophisticated transla-
tors of vibration (your five physical senses)
to interpret your physical life experience,
you were also born with other sensors—
your emotions—that are further
vibrational interpreters that help you
understand, in the moment, the
experiences that you
are living.

OCTOBER 25

When
you say, "I want
this thing to happen that
hasn't happened yet," you are
not only activating the vibration of
your desire, but you are also activating
a vibration of the absence of your
desire—so nothing changes for you.
And often, even when you do not speak
the second part of the sentence, and you
say only, "I want this to happen," there
is an unspoken vibration within you
that continues to hold you in a
state of not allowing your
desire.

Your emotions
are your indicators of the
vibrational content of your
Being, in every moment. And so, when
you become aware of the feeling of your
emotions, you can also be aware of your
vibrational offering. And once you combine
your knowledge of the *Law of Attraction* with
your in-this-moment awareness of what your
vibrational offering is, then you will have
full control of your own powerful point of
attraction—and with this knowledge,
you can now guide your life
experience in any way
you choose.

OCTOBER 24

As you are *Segment Intending* throughout a day, you will feel the power and the momentum of your intentions building; you will find yourself feeling gloriously invincible; you will feel as if there is nothing that you cannot be, do, or have as you are seeing yourself again and again in creative control of your own life experience.

Your
emotions indicate
the degree of your align-
ment with Source, and although
you can never disconnect from it
altogether, the thoughts you choose to
give your attention to do give you a substan-
tial range in alignment or misalignment with
the Non-Physical Energy that is truly who-
you-are. And so, with time and practice, you
will come to know, in every moment, your
degree of alignment with who-you-really-
are, for when you are in full allowance of
the Energy of your Source, you thrive;
and to the degree that you do not
allow this alignment, you
do not thrive.

The value of the
Segment Intending Process
is to encourage you to pause
many times during the day to say,
"This is what I want from this
period of my life experience. I want it
and I expect it." And as you set forth
those powerful words, you become
what we call a *Selective Sifter*—
you attract into your experience what you want.

MARCH 11

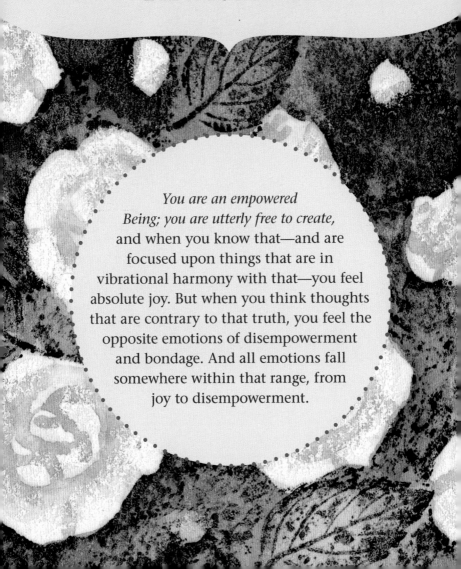

*You are an empowered
Being; you are utterly free to create,*
and when you know that—and are
focused upon things that are in
vibrational harmony with that—you feel
absolute joy. But when you think thoughts
that are contrary to that truth, you feel the
opposite emotions of disempowerment
and bondage. And all emotions fall
somewhere within that range, from
joy to disempowerment.

We encourage
an application of the
Segment Intending Process when
you are already feeling good. If
you are feeling bad, in this moment,
do something else in order to improve
your current mood and point of
attraction. And then, once you are
feeling better, you could return
to this powerful *Segment
Intending Process.*

In the same way
that sculptors mold clay
into the creation that pleases
them, you create by molding Energy.
You mold it through your power of
focus—by thinking about things, remembering things, and imagining things. You
focus the Energy when you speak, when
you write, when you listen, when you
are silent, when you remember, and
when you imagine—you focus
it through the projection
of thought.

OCTOBER 21

If you want many
things all at the same time,
it adds confusion. But when
you only focus upon the specifics of
what you want in any particular moment, you bring to your creation clarity and
power—and therefore, speed. And that is the
point of *Segment Intending:* to stop, as you are
entering a new Segment, and to identify what
it is you most want so that you may give your
attention to (and therefore draw power unto)
that. *Segment Intending* will put you in the
position of being a deliberate, magnetic attractor, or creator, in each of
your Segments throughout
your day.

MARCH 13

The Creative Process is conceptually a simple one. It consists of just three steps:

Step 1 (your work): You ask.

Step 2 (not your work): The answer is given.

Step 3 (your work): The answer, which has been given, must be received or allowed (you have to let it in).

For some, you may find it more efficient and effective to carry a small notebook and physically stop and identify the Segment while you write a list of your intentions in your notebook—for as you are writing, you will find yourself at your strongest point of clarity and at your strongest point of focus—and so, in the beginning of your deliberate *Segment Intending,* you may find a notebook a very great and valuable asset.

MARCH 14

All things that
you ask for, large and small,
are immediately understood and
fully offered, without exception.
Every point of Consciousness has the
right and the ability to ask, and all points of
Consciousness are honored and responded to
immediately. When you ask, it is given—every
time! Your "asking" is sometimes spoken with
your words, but more often it emanates from
you vibrationally as a constant stream of
personally honed preferences, each
building on the next, and each
one respected and answered.

OCTOBER 19

You enter a new
Segment anytime your
intentions change: If you are
washing dishes and the telephone
rings, you enter a new Segment. When
you get into your vehicle, you enter a new
Segment. When another person walks into
the room, you enter a new Segment. If you will
take the time to get your thought of expectation started even before you are inside your
new Segment, you will be able to set the
tone of the Segment more specifically
than if you walk into the Segment
and begin to observe it as it
already is.

MARCH 15

Every subject is really two
subjects: There is that which
you desire, and the lack of it.
Often—even when you believe you
are thinking about something that
you desire—you are actually thinking about the exact opposite of
what you desire.

OCTOBER 18

You are actually
prepaving your future
experiences constantly without
even knowing you are doing so.
You are continually projecting your
expectations into your future
experiences, and so a process of
Segment Intending will help you to
consciously consider what you are
projecting—and it will help to
give you control of your
future Segments.

MARCH 16

What you think
and what you get is always
a perfect vibrational match, so it
can be very helpful to make a conscious correlation between what you
are thinking and what is manifesting in
your life experience; but it is even more
helpful if you are able to discern where
you are headed even before you get there.
Once you understand your emotions
and what your vibrational offering
has been, you can tell, by the
way you feel, exactly where
you are headed.

OCTOBER 17

If you are experiencing a physical condition that has your attention, you are, through your attention to your current condition, projecting it on into your future experience. But, by focusing on a *different* future experience, you are now activating that *different* experience; and as you project that changed experience into your future, you leave your current experience behind.

MARCH 17

You are not
always aware that your
desires have been answered
because there is often a time gap
between your *asking* and your *allowing*.
Even though a clear desire has emanated as
a result of the contrast you have considered,
you often, rather than giving your attention
purely to the desire itself, focus back on the
contrasting situation that gave birth to the
desire—and in doing so, your vibration
is more about the reason you have
launched the desire than about
the desire itself.

OCTOBER 16

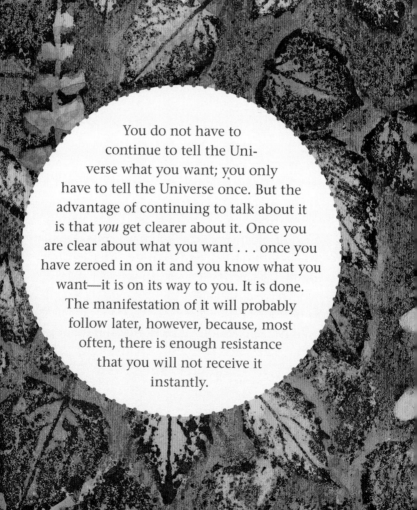

You do not have to continue to tell the Universe what you want; you only have to tell the Universe once. But the advantage of continuing to talk about it is that *you* get clearer about it. Once you are clear about what you want . . . once you have zeroed in on it and you know what you want—it is on its way to you. It is done. The manifestation of it will probably follow later, however, because, most often, there is enough resistance that you will not receive it instantly.

With each state-
ment of need and justi-
fication, you unwittingly rein-
force the vibration of your current
unpleasant situation, and in doing
so, you continue to hold yourself out
of vibrational alignment with your new
desire and out of the receiving mode of
what you are asking for. . . . *As long as
you are more aware of what you <u>do not</u>
want regarding a situation, what
you <u>do</u> want cannot come
to you.*

OCTOBER 15

In the moment
that you say "I prefer"
or "I like" or "I appreciate" or
"I want," the heavens part for you,
and the Non-Physical Energies, in that
instant, begin orchestrating the manifestation of your desire. In that instant! Faster
than you can speak it, the Energy begins to
flow, and circumstances and events (in an
orchestration that we cannot begin to
describe) begin to fall into place in order
to give you exactly what you want—
and if it were not for your resistance, things would happen
really fast.

Once you under-
stand that the way you *feel*
indicates your level of *allowing* or
resisting, you now hold the key to creating anything that you desire. It is not
possible for you to consistently feel positive emotion about something and have it
turn out badly, just as it is not possible for
you to consistently feel bad about something and have it turn out well—and
the way you feel will tell you if
you are allowing your natural
Well-Being or not.

OCTOBER 14

If you regurgitate your script often enough, you begin to accept it as reality; and when you are accepting it in the way you accept reality, the Universe believes it and responds in the same way.

We refer to the
Non-Physical You as your
Inner Being, or your *Source.* It is
not important what you call that
Source of Energy, or *Life Force,* but it *is*
important that you are consciously aware
of when you are allowing a full Connection to it and when you are restricting it
in some way—and your emotions are
your constant indicators of your
degree of allowing or resisting
that Connection.

Scripting is one of those processes that we offer to assist you in telling the Universe the way you want it to be. *Scripting* will help you break your habit of talking about things as they are, and will help you begin talking about how you would like things to be. *Scripting* will help you offer your vibration *deliberately*.

As you con-
sciously consider the way
you will get better
and better at directing the Source
Energy, and you will become a dis-
ciplined and joyous *Deliberate Creator*.
With practice, you will be able to achieve
a focused control of this *Creative Energy;*
and, like the skilled sculptor, you will
take delight in the molding of this
Energy that creates worlds, and
direct it toward your individ-
ual creative endeavors.

You are the
vibrational writer of the
script of your life—and everyone else in the Universe is playing
the part that you have assigned to
them. You can literally script any life
that you desire, and the Universe will
deliver to you the essence of the people,
places, and events just as you decide
them to be. For you are the creator
of your own experience—you
have only to decide it and
allow it to be.

When you are
thinking about something
that you have been wanting for a
very long time—and you are noticing
that it has not yet happened—a strong
negative emotion would be present within
you. However, if you are thinking about
something that you have been wanting—and
you are imagining that it *is* happening—
then your emotion would be one of anticipation or eagerness. And so, you can tell
by the way you *feel* whether you are,
in this moment, allowing or
resisting your desire.

OCTOBER 11

The *Scripting Process* will help you be more specific about your desires, and, with that greater clarity about exactly what you *do* desire, you will feel the power of this specific focus. The longer you concentrate on a subject, and the more detail you give to it, the faster the Energy moves. And, with practice, you can actually *feel* the momentum of your desire; you can *feel* the Universal Forces converging. Often, you will be able to know when you are on the brink of a breakthrough or a manifestation just by virtue of the way you feel.

We are not
encouraging you to
make an effort to *control* your
thoughts, but instead, to make
an effort to more or less *guide* your
thoughts. And it is not even so much
about guiding your thoughts as it is
about reaching for a *feeling,* because
reaching for the way you would like
to *feel* is an easier way to hold your
thoughts in vibrational alignment with that which you
believe is good.

OCTOBER 10

This is how the *Scripting Process* works: Pretend that you are a writer and that whatever you write will be performed exactly as you write it. Your only job is to describe, in detail, everything, exactly as you want it to be.

MARCH 24

Whenever you have con-
sistently focused upon a subject,
causing a consistent vibrational
activation of it within you, it becomes
a practiced or dominant thought. *And
once your focused attention has sufficiently
activated a dominant vibration within
you, things—wanted or unwanted—will
begin to make their way into your
personal experience. It is <u>Law.</u>*

OCTOBER 9

You can look
at this in two different
ways: *If I do such and such, these
good things will happen*, or *If I don't
do such and such, these bad things will
happen*. The first *inspires* you to action
from a positive place. The second *moti-
vates* you to action from a negative place.
Your *Book of Positive Aspects* will put
you more and more in the position of
attracting—by virtue of your
inspired positive feeling—
whatever you desire.

Before you can
effectively benefit from
paying attention to your emotions, you must first accept that
Well-Being is the only Stream that flows.
You can allow or disallow this Stream,
but when you allow it, you feel well; and
when you disallow it, you feel sick. In
other words, there is only a Stream of
wellness, which you are allowing or
resisting, and you can tell by the
way you *feel* which you
are doing.

If we were
standing in your physical
shoes, we would not let
the *reality* of something be our
basis for attention; we would let the
feeling-vibration of it be our basis. So we
would start saying, to anyone who was
interested in knowing what we were
about, "If it feels good, I give it my full
attention; if it doesn't, I don't look at
it at all." *You can and will create the
essence of anything that you are
giving your attention to.*

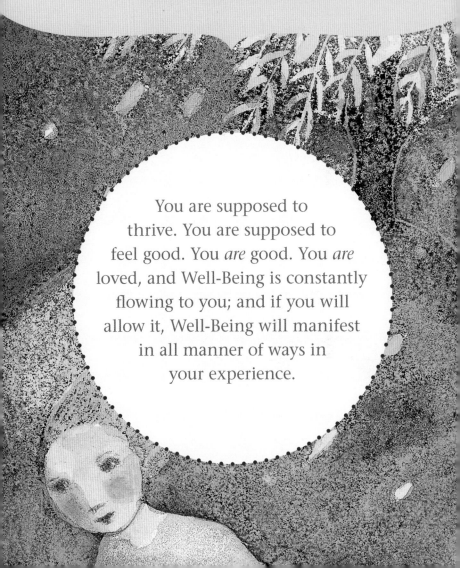

MARCH 26

You are supposed to
thrive. You are supposed to
feel good. You *are* good. You *are*
loved, and Well-Being is constantly
flowing to you; and if you will
allow it, Well-Being will manifest
in all manner of ways in
your experience.

OCTOBER 7

We want to encourage
you to give more of your attention to what makes you feel good—
not something so radical that you
must control every thought—*just make
a decision that you will look for what you
want to see.* It is not a difficult decision to make, but it can make a big
difference in what you bring
into your experience.

A *belief* is only a
practiced vibration. In other
words, once you have practiced a
thought long enough, then, anytime
you approach the subject of that thought,
the *Law of Attraction* will take you easily
into the full vibration of your belief. And so,
as you have a life experience that matches
those thoughts you were pondering, you
conclude, "Yes, this is truth." And while
it may be accurate to call it "truth,"
we would prefer to call it
attraction or *creation*.

If, when you
focus upon what you
want, you would feel good; and
if, when you feel good, you would
be in the positive mode of attraction,
then would not your most important
work be to look for the positive aspects
of all things, to look for the parts
of all things that are uplifting to
you—and to get your attention
off of any potholes in
the streets?

MARCH 28

Anything that you give
your attention to will become
your "truth." The *Law of
Attraction* says that it must. Your
life, and everyone else's, too, is but a
reflection of the predominance
of your thoughts. There is no
exception to this.

The benefits of your *Book of Positive Aspects Process* will be many: You will feel wonderful during the process. Your point of attraction will continue to improve, no matter how good it is now. Your relationship with each subject that you write about will become richer and more satisfying—and the *Law of Attraction* will deliver even more wonderful people, places, experiences, and things for you to enjoy.

To be the *Deliberate Creator of your own experience,* you will be one who has decided to direct your thoughts, for only when you deliberately choose the direction of your thoughts can you deliberately affect your own point of attraction. You cannot continue to discuss, observe, and believe things in the same way you always have—and make changes in your point of attraction—any more (as we mentioned previously) than you can set your radio dial to 630AM and receive the broadcast from 101FM. Your vibrational frequencies have to match.

The more *positive aspects* you search for, the more you are going to find; and the more *positive aspects* you find, the more you will search for more. In the *Book of Positive Aspects Process,* you will activate within yourself a high vibration of Well-Being (which matches who-you-really-are). And you will feel wonderful. And even better, this vibration will become so practiced that it will become your dominant vibration—and all aspects of your experience will now begin to reflect this higher vibration.

MARCH 30

When fully
focused upon your desire
(and your vibrational offering
purely reflects that), you feel wonderful. And when focused upon the absence
of something you truly want, you feel awful.
Your emotions always let you know what you
are doing with your vibration; your emotions
always let you know exactly what your point
of attraction is; and so, by paying attention to
your emotions and by *deliberately* offering
thoughts that affect the way you feel, you
can *consciously* guide yourself into the
vibrational frequency that will
allow the fulfillment of any
desire you hold.

Gently and easily, begin writing down the thoughts that come to you in response to your *Positive Aspects* Questions. Do not try to force these ideas, but let them flow easily through you onto your paper. Write as long as the good-feeling thoughts flow, and then read what you have written, enjoying your own words. Now, turn to the next page and write another name or title of someone or something that you feel good about, and then repeat the process until about 20 minutes have passed.

MARCH 31

Once you begin
to accept yourself as a
Vibrational Being who attracts
all things that come into your
experience, and once you understand
the correlation between what you are
thinking and feeling and what you are
receiving—then you hold the keys
to get from wherever you are to
wherever you want to be, on
all subjects.

OCTOBER 2

At the top of
the first page of your
Positive Aspects notebook, write
the name, or a brief description, of
someone or something that you always
feel good about. It could be the name of
your lovable cat, your best friend, or the
person you are in love with. It could be the
name of your favorite city or restaurant.
And as you focus upon the name or title
that you have written, ask yourself
these questions: *What do I like
about you? Why do I love you so
much? What are your
positive aspects?*

Most people do
not believe that they have
control over what they believe.
They observe things happening
around them and evaluate them, but
they usually feel that they have no control whatsoever about the belief that is
formulating within them. They spend their
lives sorting events into categories of good
or bad, wanted or unwanted, right or
wrong—but rarely do they understand
that they have the ability to control their personal relationship
with these events.

To begin the process of the *Book of Positive Aspects:* Purchase a notebook that feels good when you hold it in your hands. Because of the action that will be involved in this process, not only is an improved degree of focus certain, but with the focus will come an increase in both your clarity and in your feeling of being alive. Now, on the cover of your notebook write: *My Book of Positive Aspects.*

APRIL 2

Through personal
force, or gathering in groups
to gain the feeling of more power,
many people seek to preserve their own
Well-Being by attempting to take control
of any circumstances that they believe could
threaten it. But in this attraction-based Universe where there is no such thing as exclusion,
the harder they push against unwanted things,
the more they achieve vibrational alignment
with unwanted things—and, in doing so, the
more they invite unwanted things into their
own experience. . . . The more you
defend your own beliefs, the more
the *Law of Attraction* helps you
live them out.

SEPTEMBER 30

As a result of
the influence surrounding
you, you may be flowing Energy
toward financial disaster, or toward a
body that will not function well. As such,
your *Inner Being,* which is aware of what you
are projecting into your future, may offer you
a dream showing you where you are going.
And so, you awaken and you think, *Ah, I don't
want that!* And then you say, *What is it I <u>do</u>
want? And <u>why</u> do I want it?* And then you
start flowing your Energy productively
toward what you do want, and
thereby changing your future
experience.

By paying
enough attention to any-
thing, the essence of what you
have been giving thought to will eventually become a physical manifestation.
And then as others observe your physical
manifestation, through their attention to it
they help it to expand. And then, in time,
this manifestation, whether it is one that is
wanted or not, is called "Truth." Deliberate Creation is about deliberately
choosing those experiences you
make your Truths.

Your dreams are manifestations of your vibrational point of attraction, so you can evaluate your dreams to determine what you are really doing with your vibration. Your dreams are, sort of, a sneak preview of the essence of that which is to come—so if you evaluate the content of your dream, you can often determine what your point of attraction is—and then if you do not wish to live out the dream you have been dreaming, you can do something about changing it.

When your newly activated thoughts are general and not very focused, those vibrations are still very small and do not yet have much attraction power; and so, in these early stages, you would not likely see any manifested evidence of your attention to the subject. But as the thought gains momentum, you now begin to get an emotional reading on how well this growing thought-vibration is matching the Energy of your Source. If it matches who-you-are, your good-feeling emotions indicate that. If it does *not* match who-you-are, your bad-feeling emotions indicate that.

SEPTEMBER 28

Sometimes when you have
wanted something for a long
while but you do not see any way
for it to really happen, you will experience a dream where it *does* happen.
And then, in the pleasant recollection
of the dream, you soften your vibration of resistance—and then your
desire can be fulfilled.

APRIL 5

When you con-
tinue to focus upon any
thought, it becomes increas-
ingly easy to continue to focus
upon it because the *Law of Attraction*
is making more thoughts like it available to you. Emotionally speaking,
you are developing a mood or an
attitude. Vibrationally speaking,
you are achieving a habitual
vibrational groove, so to
speak—or a *set-point*.

SEPTEMBER 27

Dreams can give
you a wonderful insight
into your current vibrational
state of being. Your recall of a dream
is your physical translation of blocks
of Non-Physical thought that you have
interacted with in your dream state. When
you sleep, you reemerge into the Energy of
the Non-Physical, and you have conversations (not conversations in words, but
vibrational ones). Then, as you are
awakening, you translate that block
of thought back into its
physical equivalent.

Your *emotional
set-points* can change from
not feeling good to feeling good,
for your set-points are achieved
simply by paying attention to a subject
and through your practiced thought. And
we want you to understand the extreme
value in deliberately achieving your own
set-points, because, once you expect
something, it will come. The details of
it may play out differently, but the
vibrational essence will always
be an exact match.

SEPTEMBER 26

You do not create while
you are dreaming. Your dream
is a manifestation of what you
have been thinking during your
awake state. However, once you are
awake and you are now thinking
about, or discussing, your dream—
those thoughts do affect your
future creations.

Every living thing—animal, human, or plant—experiences that which is called *death*, with no exception. Spirit, which is who-we-really-are, is Eternal. So what death must be is but a changing of the perspective of that Eternal Spirit. If you are standing in your physical body and consciously connected to that Spirit, then you are Eternal in nature and you need never fear any "endedness," because, from that perspective, there is none. (You will never cease to be, for you are Eternal Consciousness.)

SEPTEMBER 25

"How did I feel
as that was happening?"
If you have awakened from a
very good-feeling dream, you can be
confident that your dominant thoughts
surrounding that subject are pointed toward
manifestations that you *do* want. When you
awaken from a bad-feeling dream, know that
your dominant thoughts are in the process of
attracting something that you do *not* want;
however—*no matter where you stand, in terms
of what is manifesting in your experience,
you can always make a new decision
and change the manifestation to
something that is even more
pleasing.*

Your emotions let you know how much Source Energy you are summoning, in this moment, by virtue of the desire you hold in this moment. They also let you know whether your preponderance of thought on the subject matches your desire, or matches the absence of your desire. For example, a feeling of passion or enthusiasm indicates that there is a very strong desire focused in the moment. A feeling of rage or revenge also indicates that there is a very strong desire; however, a feeling of lethargy or boredom indicates very little focused desire in the moment.

You must give
significant attention to
any subject for it to become
powerful enough to manifest in your
experience, and quite a bit of attention
must also be given to a subject before
it will begin to show up in your dream
state. For that reason, your more meaning-
ful dreams are always accompanied by
strong emotion; the emotion may feel
good or bad—but it will always be
strong enough so that you will
recognize the feeling.

When you really, really want something, are thinking about your desire, and are feeling pleasure from the thought, your current thought-vibration is in alignment with your desire—and we call that: *allowing*. But when you really, really want something and are feeling anger, fear, or disappointment, that means you are focused upon the opposite of your desire; and, in doing so, you are introducing another non-matching vibration to the mix—and we call that: *resistance*. The degree of negative emotion that you are experiencing indicates the degree of your resistance to your receiving your desire.

SEPTEMBER 23

Although you
may be able to recall
different aspects of your
dream state throughout the day,
usually the best chance of recalling
your dreams is when you first awaken.
And as you begin to recall one of your
dreams, relax and try to remember how
you *felt* during the dream sequence,
for recalling your *emotions* will give
you even more important information than recalling the
details of your dream.

Your emotions
are *absolute* indicators of
your vibrational content. Therefore, they are the perfect reflection of
your current point of attraction. Emotions help you know, in any moment,
whether or not you are currently allowing
the fulfillment of your desire. . . . *It is
our encouragement that you pay attention
to how you feel and allow your
emotions to be the valuable
indicators they are.*

SEPTEMBER 22

The process for evaluating dreams is as follows: As you go to bed, consciously acknowledge that your dreams accurately reflect your thoughts. Say to yourself, *It is my intention to rest well and to awaken refreshed. And if there is anything important for me to recall from my dream state, I will recall it when I awaken.* As you awaken, before you get up, lie there for a few minutes and ask yourself, *Do I remember anything from my dream state?*

A negative feeling
indicates that your current
choice of thoughts is so out of
harmony with your Source Energy that
you are disallowing your full connection
to that Energy Stream. (You could say that
your fuel tank is approaching empty.) Your
emotions do not create, but they do indicate
what you are currently attracting. If your
emotions help you know that your choice of
thoughts is not taking you in the direction
that you desire to go, then do something about that: *Replenish your
connection by choosing better-
feeling thoughts.*

SEPTEMBER 21

If you are in the process of creating something that you do *not* want, it would be easier to change the direction of your thoughts *before* it manifests than waiting to change your thoughts until *after* it manifests.

You have the ability to direct your own thoughts; you have the option of observing things as they are, or of imagining them as you want them to be—and whichever option you choose, whether you are imagining or observing, is equally powerful. In every case, your thoughts produce a vibration within you that equals your point of attraction—and then, circumstances and events line up to match the vibrations that you have offered.

SEPTEMBER 20

The essence of the way
you feel about the things you
think about most will eventually
manifest in your real-life experience—
but it takes even *less* time and attention
for it to manifest in your dream state.
And for that reason, *your dreams can be
of immense value in helping you understand what you are in the process of
creating in your awake state.*

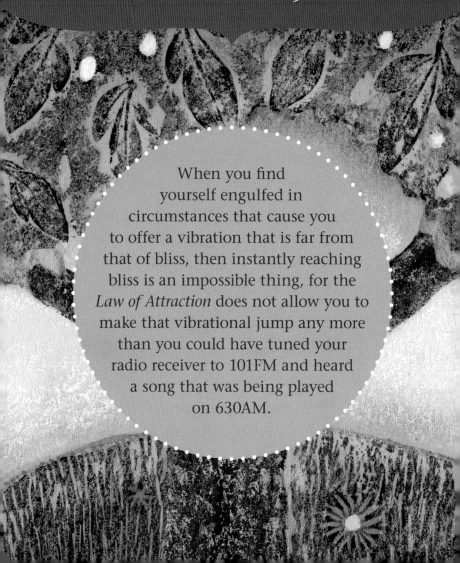

When you find
yourself engulfed in
circumstances that cause you
to offer a vibration that is far from
that of bliss, then instantly reaching
bliss is an impossible thing, for the
Law of Attraction does not allow you to
make that vibrational jump any more
than you could have tuned your
radio receiver to 101FM and heard
a song that was being played
on 630AM.

When
you dream about
something, it is always a
match to the thoughts that you
have been thinking, and so—*since
each of your dreams is, in fact, your
creation*—it is not possible for you to
dream about anything that you have
not created through your thoughts.
The fact that it has now manifested
in your dream state means that
you have given it a sig-
nificant amount of
thought.

It is not a dif-
ficult thing to change
the pattern of your vibration,
especially when you understand
that you can do it a little bit at a time.
Once you have an understanding of
how vibrations work, how they affect
your experience, and, most important,
what your emotions are telling you
about your vibrations, now you can
make steady, fast progress toward
the achievement of anything
that you desire.

SEPTEMBER 18

What you think about and
what manifests in your life
experience is always a vibrational
match; and, in the same way, what
you think about and what manifests in your dream state is always
a vibrational match.

It is not your
job to *make* something
happen—Universal Forces
are in place for all of that. Your
work is to simply determine what
you want. . . . *If we were standing in
your physical shoes, our attention would
be upon bringing ourselves into alignment with the desires and preferences
that we have launched—we would
<u>consciously</u> feel our way
into alignment.*

Things little and
things big, things that
you would call extraordinary
and significant, and things that you
would call not very significant—*everything that you have ever identified that you
have ever wanted will be lined up right outside
your door* . . . and, in the moment that you
open the door, all things wanted will
flow to you. And then we will hold
a seminar on "How to Deal with
Manifestations of All This Stuff
That Is Flowing In."

All of your desires, wants,
or preferences emanate from
you naturally and constantly, for
you stand at the Leading Edge of a
Universe that makes that so. So, you
cannot hold your desires back;
the Eternal nature of this
Universe insists that your
desires come forth.

SEPTEMBER 16

We sort of see you from an aerial view, and it is like you are standing on one side of a closed door, and on the other side are all the things you have been wanting, just leaning up against the door, waiting for you to open it. They have been there from the first moment you asked for them: your lovers, your perfect bodies, your ideal jobs, all the money that you could ever imagine—all the things that you have ever wanted!

Regarding your creation of your own life experience, *there really is only one important question for you to ask:* "How can I bring myself into vibrational alignment with the desires that my experience has produced?" *And the answer is simple:* Pay attention to the way you feel, and deliberately choose thoughts—about everything— that feel good to you when you think them.

SEPTEMBER 15

Within 30 days of mild effort, you can go from being one of the most resistant people on the planet to one of the *least* resistant people on the planet—and then, those who are watching you will be amazed by the number of manifestations that begin to occur in your physical experience.

As you made the decision to come into this body, you knew that you were a creator and that the Earth environment would inspire your specific creation. You also knew that whenever you asked, it would be given. And you were thrilled by the prospect of being inspired to attain your own specific desires, understanding that Source would flow through you to achieve the completion of those desires.

SEPTEMBER 14

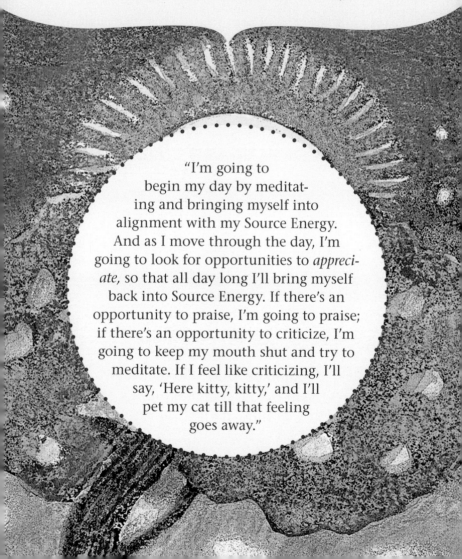

"I'm going to begin my day by meditating and bringing myself into alignment with my Source Energy. And as I move through the day, I'm going to look for opportunities to *appreciate*, so that all day long I'll bring myself back into Source Energy. If there's an opportunity to praise, I'm going to praise; if there's an opportunity to criticize, I'm going to keep my mouth shut and try to meditate. If I feel like criticizing, I'll say, 'Here kitty, kitty,' and I'll pet my cat till that feeling goes away."

We refer to the time between your offering of a thought and its physical manifestation as "the buffer of time." It is that wonderful time of offering thought . . . noticing how it feels . . . adjusting the thought to achieve an even better feeling . . . and then, in an attitude of absolute expectation, enjoying the gentle, steady unfolding of anything and everything that you have concluded as your desires.

SEPTEMBER 13

Do you know that
you could have every deadly
disease known to man (and some
they have not even figured out yet) in
your body right now, and tomorrow they
could all be gone if—from one day to the
next—you learned how to allow the Energy to
flow? We are really not encouraging those kinds
of quantum leaps; they're a little uncomfortable. What we *are* really encouraging is that,
every day, you be selfish enough to say,
"Nothing is more important than that
I feel good. And I'm going to find
ways to do so today."

APRIL 20

There is never a reason for
you to be without something
that you desire. Nor is there ever a
reason for you to experience something
that you do not desire—for you hold absolute control of your experiences. We want
you to know that you always hold the power
and control of your own life experience. The
only reason why you could ever experience
something other than what you desire is
because you are giving the majority of
your attention to something other
than what *you* desire.

Everything that happens to you and everything that happens to everyone you know occurs because of the Energy that you are summoning and allowing or not allowing. Everything is about that relationship with Energy. Everyone you know who is having every experience that you know, is having it because of the focused desire that their life has brought to them and the state of *allowing* or *resistance* that they're in at any moment.

The *Law of Attraction* always yields to you the essence of the balance of your thoughts. No exceptions. You get what you think about—whether you want it or not. And, in time, and with practice, you will come to remember that the *Law of Attraction* is always consistent. It never tricks you; it never deceives you; it never confuses you, for the *Law of Attraction* responds precisely to the vibration that you are offering.

SEPTEMBER 11

"Well, what if I've really developed major habits of negativity? Is 15 minutes going to change that?" *Probably not right away. But the next time you go to one of those negative thoughts, you are going to be more aware of it. Your <u>Guidance System</u> is going to be stimulated so that you will be aware—probably for the first time in your life—of what you are doing with your Non-Physical Energy.*

The basis of
your world is one of Well-
Being. You can allow it or not,
but the basis is Well-Being. The *Law
of Attraction* says: *That which is like
unto itself, is drawn.* And so, the essence
of whatever you give your attention
to is unfolding in your experience.
Therefore, there is nothing that
you cannot be, do, or have.
This is *Law.*

You cannot be part of this physical environment without endless desires being born within you. And as these desires are being born within you, the Universe is answering them. And now, because of 15 minutes of *allowing,* whether you were petting the cat, practicing your breathing in meditation, listening to a waterfall or soothing music, or were on a *Rampage of Appreciation* . . . during that time of *allowing* you established a vibration that no longer caused resistance to the things that you have been asking for.

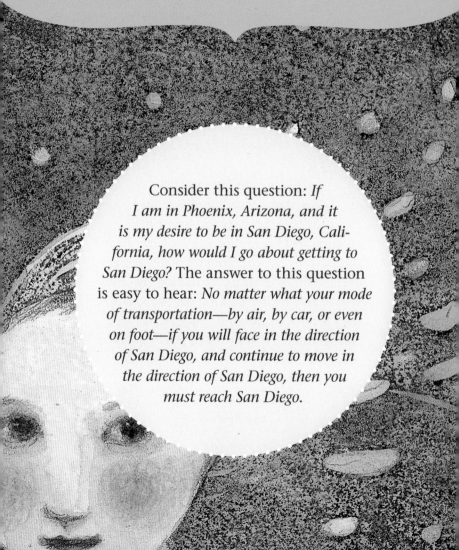

Consider this question: *If I am in Phoenix, Arizona, and it is my desire to be in San Diego, California, how would I go about getting to San Diego?* The answer to this question is easy to hear: *No matter what your mode of transportation—by air, by car, or even on foot—if you will face in the direction of San Diego, and continue to move in the direction of San Diego, then you must reach San Diego.*

A big benefit from meditation that you will notice right away is that things you have been wanting will begin showing up. Now, why is this? Why does 15 minutes of just being, set those kinds of things in motion? Because you have already been asking, and now, during your time of meditation, you have stopped the resistance that has been holding it at bay. Because of your practiced meditation, you are now *allowing* your desires to flow into your experience.

Once you
understand the clarity that
your emotions provide, you will
never again not know what you are
doing with your current thought. You
will always be aware of whether you are, in
this moment, moving toward or away from
your intended goal or desire. Your awareness
of the way you feel will give you the clarity you have been seeking. Once you have
the knowledge that you are moving in
the direction of your desires, you
may begin to relax a little bit
and enjoy your fantastic
journey.

Meditation is a
state of *allowing* where, for
just a few moments, you stop
trying to make anything happen. It
is a time when you are saying to your
Source Energy, to your *Inner Being,* to your
God (or whatever you want to call it): *Here
I am, in a state of allowing Source Energy to
flow purely through me.* Fifteen minutes of
effort will change your life. It will
allow the Energy that is natural to
you to flow; you will feel better in
the moment, and you will feel
more energized when you
come out of it.

You are a perfect yet expanding Being, in a perfect yet expanding world. Your expansion is a given, the expansion of your time-space reality is a given, and the expansion of this Universe is a given—it is just ever so much more satisfying for you to consciously and deliberately participate in your own expansion.

SEPTEMBER 7

For 10 or 15 min-
utes every day, we would
quiet our mind in meditation;
we would close our eyes; we would be
aware of breathing air into our lungs; and
our intention would be nothing more than
being in this moment and being consciously
aware of our breathing . . . nothing to do other
than breathe—not fixing breakfast, not comb-
ing hair, not wondering how someone is
doing, not thinking about yesterday, not
worrying about tomorrow, not focusing
on anything in this moment except
air in and air out.

If you have the ability
to imagine it, or even to think
about it, this Universe has the
ability and the resources to deliver
it fully unto you, for this Universe
is like a well-stocked kitchen with
every ingredient imaginable
at your disposal.

SEPTEMBER 6

If we were in your physical shoes, we would sit quietly, by ourselves, in some pleasant place where we would not be interrupted—maybe under a tree, maybe in our vehicle, maybe in the bathroom or garden—and we would utilize 10 or 15 minutes, and not much more time than that, to quiet our mind in meditation.

Without the abil-
ity to know what you do *not*
want, you could not know what
you *do* want. And so, it is through your
exposure to life experience that your natural preferences are born. In fact, these preferences are exuding from you in all moments
of every day, at many levels of your Being.
Even the cells of your well-tended-to body are
having their own experience and are ema-
nating *their* own preferences—and every
preference is recognized by Source and
immediately answered, with
no exceptions.

SEPTEMBER 5

There are other
ways of raising your vibrations than meditation, such as
listening to music that makes your
heart sing, jogging in a beautiful place,
petting your cat, walking your dog, and so
on. Often you are in your highest state of connection to Source Energy while you are driving
your vehicle. Your goal is to release any thought
that causes resistance so that you are then in a
place of pure, positive thought. Just find any
thought that feels good when you think
it, and practice it until you begin to set
that tone within you—and then,
other good-feeling thoughts
will follow.

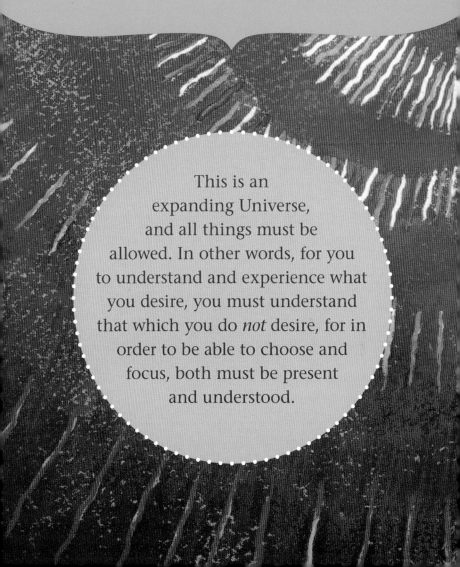

APRIL 28

This is an expanding Universe, and all things must be allowed. In other words, for you to understand and experience what you desire, you must understand that which you do *not* desire, for in order to be able to choose and focus, both must be present and understood.

SEPTEMBER 4

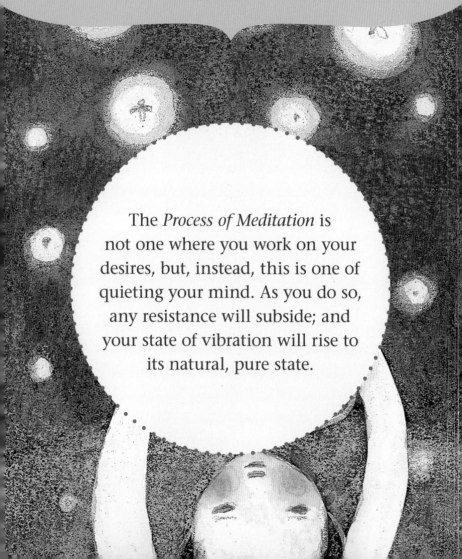

The *Process of Meditation* is
not one where you work on your
desires, but, instead, this is one of
quieting your mind. As you do so,
any resistance will subside; and
your state of vibration will rise to
its natural, pure state.

APRIL 29

Every physical Being on your
Planet is your partner in co-
creation, and if you would accept
that and appreciate the diversity
of beliefs and desires—all of you
would have more expansive,
satisfying, and fulfilling
experiences.

SEPTEMBER 3

With an understanding of the *Laws of the Universe* and some willingness to deliberately choose thoughts, you can, in time, replace all hindering beliefs with life-giving beliefs; but there is a process that can give you the immediate benefit of changing your beliefs, in a much shorter time—we call this the *Process of Meditation*.

Imagine yourself
as a chef in an extremely
well-stocked kitchen that con-
tains every imaginable ingredient,
and as you proceed, there are many
ingredients that are *not* appropriate for
your creation, so you do not utilize them,
but you also feel no discomfort about their
existence. You simply utilize the ingredients that *will* enhance your creation—
and you leave the ingredients that
are not appropriate for your
creation out of your pie.

Any thought
that you continue to think
is called a *belief*. And many of
your beliefs serve you extremely
well: thoughts that harmonize with the
knowledge of your Source, and thoughts
that match the desires that you hold. . . .
But some of your beliefs do *not* serve you
well: Thoughts about your own inad-
equacy or your unworthiness are
examples of those kinds
of thoughts.

MAY 1

From your Non-Physical perspective, you understood that there is room enough in this expansive Universe for all manner of thought and experience. You had every intention of being deliberate about your own creative control of your own life experience and your own creations—but you had no intention of trying to control the creations of others.

SEPTEMBER 1

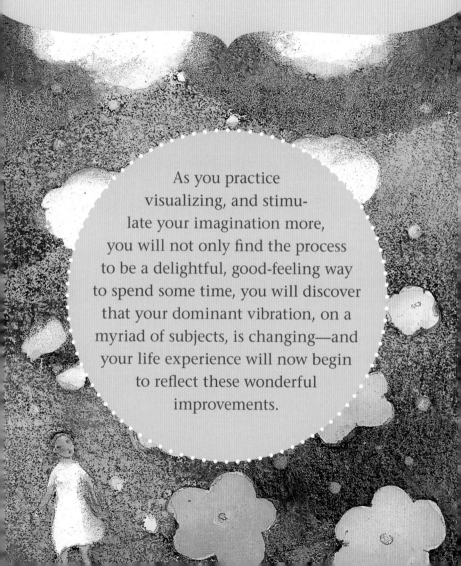

As you practice visualizing, and stimulate your imagination more, you will not only find the process to be a delightful, good-feeling way to spend some time, you will discover that your dominant vibration, on a myriad of subjects, is changing—and your life experience will now begin to reflect these wonderful improvements.

MAY 2

From the variety,
or contrast, your preferences
or desires are born. And in the
moment that your preference begins to
exist, it begins to draw to itself—through
the *Law of Attraction*—the essence of that
which matches it . . . and it then begins an
immediate expansion. This is how the Universe
expands, and this is why you are on the Leading
Edge of the expansion. The valuable contrast
continues to provide the birthing of endless
new desires, and as each desire is born,
Source responds to the desire—it is a
never-ending, always flowing, pure,
positive Energy expansion.

Can you remem-
ber events that have hap-
pened? If you can remember,
then you can do *Virtual Reality*,
because none of that is right here, right
now; and as you are remembering, you
are re-creating it from something. . . .
So visualizing, or *Virtual Reality*, is no
different. It is conjuring, but with
the singular intention of pleasing
yourself as you do so.

You cannot
ever get it done because
you cannot ever cease to be,
and neither can you ever halt your
awareness. Yet, out of your awareness
will always be born another asking,
and each asking always summons
another answering. Your Eternal
nature is one of expansion—and in
that expansion is the potential
for unspeakable joy.

AUGUST 30

No matter whether you worry or rejoice in your *Virtual Reality,* you set up a vibration that the *Law of Attraction* matches.

The contrast causes new desire to be born within you; the new desire radiates from you, and as you offer the vibration of your new desire, that desire is answered—every time. When you ask, it is given. Now think about the perfection of this process: *Continuing new ideas for the improvement of your experience emanate from you constantly, and are answered constantly.* Feel the balance and perfection of your environment: *Every point of Consciousness, even the Consciousness of a cell in your body, can request an improved state of being—and get it.*

As you create scenarios
that make you feel good, you
activate a vibration that *does* feel
good, and then the *Law of Attraction* matches that vibration. *There
is nothing more important than that
you feel good—and there is nothing
better than creating images that
cause you to feel good.*

Each point of view matters; every request is granted; and as this amazing Universe unerringly expands, there is no end to the Universal resources that fulfill these requests. And there is no end to the answers to the never-ending stream of questions—and, for that reason, there is no competition.

AUGUST 28

There is no reason why
Well-Being is not pouring
into your experience—in precise detail in response to all of the
things that you have identified that
you want—other than the fact that
you are in a bad mood, or are
angry or worried about
something.

MAY 6

All desires are answered;
all requests are granted;
and no one is left unanswered,
unloved, or unfulfilled. When
you stay aligned with your Energy
Stream, you always win—and somebody else does not have to lose
for you to win—there is
always enough.

Do not use the *Virtual Reality Process* to try to improve a specific existing situation, because in your attempt to fix something, you will bring the existing vibration into your *Virtual Reality,* and in doing so, you will lose the power of the *Virtual Reality Process.*

If someone
is not receiving what
they are asking for, it is not
because there is a shortage of
resources; it can only be that the
person holding the desire is out of
alignment with their own request.
There is no shortage; there is no
lack; there is no competition for
resources—there is only the
allowing or the disallowing
of that which you are
asking for.

AUGUST 26

Virtual Reality is a process where you get to choose everything about this moment in time, just like a director in a movie would do. To begin this process, you would first decide: *Where does this scene take place?*

MAY 8

It is extremely
important that you
know where you are in relationship to where you want to be
in order to effectively move *closer*
to where you want to be. An understanding of both where you are and
where you want to be is essential
if you are to make any deliberate decisions about your
journey.

AUGUST 25

You are continually *asking*. You cannot stop *asking;* contrast is evoking the desire from you. Your real work is to find a way to be in the receiving mode. It is similar to wanting to receive a satellite or radio signal. To do so, you have to set your receiver on the same wavelength as the transmitter or you are going to get static; you are not going to get a clear signal. In like manner, you recognize the alignment of your (transmitted and received) signals by *feeling* the alignment of your emotions.

MAY 9

Often you are
pulled this way and that
in an attempt to please another,
only to discover that no matter how
hard you try, you cannot consistently
move in any pleasing direction; and so,
you not only do not please them, but
you also do not please yourself. And
because you are being pulled in so
many different directions, your
path to where you want to be
usually gets lost in
the process.

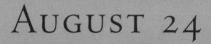

AUGUST 24

It is important
that you realize that
Steps 1 and 3 of the *Creative
Process* are different. When you
are focused upon, or praying for,
something you really want or need,
often you are not a vibrational
match *to the thing you want.*
Instead, you are a match to
the absence of *the thing
you want.*

The greatest gift
that you could ever give to
another is your own happiness,
for when you are in a state of joy
or happiness or appreciation, you are
fully connected to the Stream of pure,
positive Source Energy that is truly who-
you-are. And when you are in that state
of connection, anything or anyone
that you are holding as your object
of attention benefits from
your attention.

AUGUST 23

Remember, the *Creative Process* comprises three steps: (1) Ask (that's easy—you do it all the time). (2) Answer the asking (that is not your work—Source Energy does that). (3) Allow (be in the receiving mode of what you are asking for).

Your happiness does not depend on what others do, but only upon your own vibrational balance. And the happiness of others does not depend on you, but only upon *their* own vibrational balance, for the way anyone feels, in any moment, is only about their own mix of Energies. The way you feel is simply, clearly, and always the indicator of the vibrational balance between your desires and your vibrational offering, which, from your vantage point, you have launched.

The *Virtual Real-
ity Process* is not one where
you try to fix something that is
broken. It is one where you deliberately activate a scene in your own
mind that causes you to offer a vibration
matching the scene you have activated in
your visualization—and as you practice
visualizing pleasant scenes in your
mind, these good-feeling vibrations can then become your
new set-point.

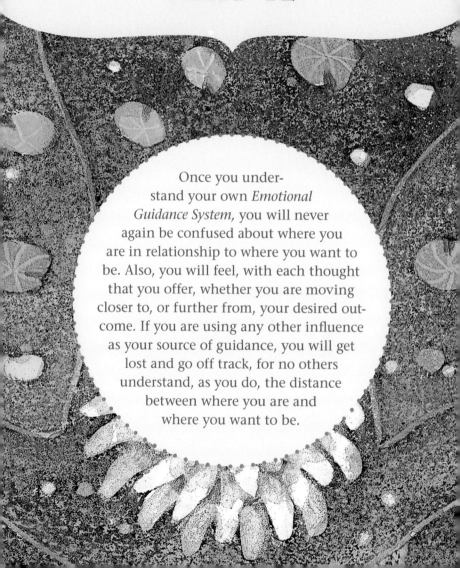

MAY 12

Once you under-
stand your own *Emotional
Guidance System*, you will never
again be confused about where you
are in relationship to where you want to
be. Also, you will feel, with each thought
that you offer, whether you are moving
closer to, or further from, your desired outcome. If you are using any other influence
as your source of guidance, you will get
lost and go off track, for no others
understand, as you do, the distance
between where you are and
where you want to be.

The Universe responds to your vibrational offering, to your point of attraction, to the thoughts you think, and to the way you feel. The Universe is not responding to what *has* been manifested in your experience, but, instead, to the vibration that you are *now* offering. The Universe makes no distinction between your actually having a million dollars and your giving thought to having a million dollars—*your point of attraction is about your thoughts, not about your manifestations.*

MAY 13

When you give
your attention to some-
thing that you desire and you
say *yes* to it, you are including it
in your vibration. But when you look
at something you do not want and you
say *no* to it, you are also including it in
your vibration. When you give no attention to it, you do not include it—but you
cannot exclude anything that you are
giving your attention to, because
your attention to it includes it in
your vibration, every time,
without exception.

Remember,
you live in a Vibrational
Universe, and all things are
managed by the *Law of Attraction*.
And you get what you think about,
whether you want it or not, because
whenever you achieve vibrational harmony with something because you are
giving it your attention, the vibrational essence of it will, in some
way, begin to show up in
your life experience.

MAY 14

There is no
thought that you can-
not eventually have—just as
there is no place that you cannot
eventually reach from wherever you
are—but you cannot instantly jump
to a thought that has a vibrational
frequency very different from
the thoughts you are usually
thinking.

AUGUST 19

We are offering processes whereby you may spend a little bit of time, every day, *intentionally* attracting into your experience good health, vitality, prosperity, and positive interactions with others—all the things that make up your vision of what the perfect life experience for you would be.

Decide to *reach for the best-feeling thought that you have access to.* A good way to feel your way up this *Vibrational Emotional Scale* is to always be reaching for the feeling of relief that comes when you release a more resistant thought and replace it with a more allowing thought. The Stream of Well-Being is *always* flowing through you; and the more you allow it, the better you feel. The more you resist it, the worse you feel.

Like a magnet,
you are attracting thoughts,
people, events, lifestyles—everything that you are living. And so, as
you see things as they are, you attract
more of the same; but as you see things
as you would like them to be, you attract
them as you would like them to be. This
is why the better it gets, the better it
gets; or the worse it gets, the worse
it gets—people tend to look
mostly at what-is.

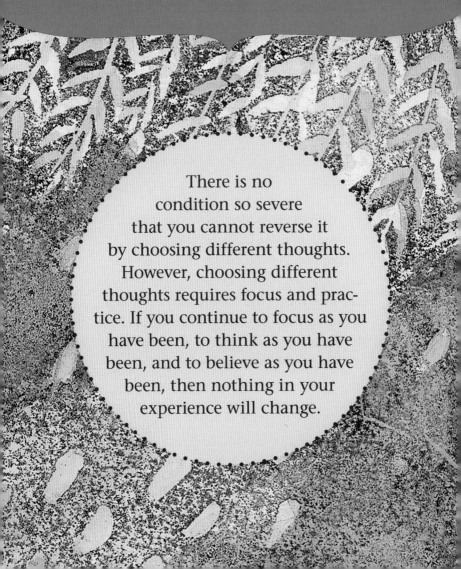

MAY 16

There is no
condition so severe
that you cannot reverse it
by choosing different thoughts.
However, choosing different
thoughts requires focus and practice. If you continue to focus as you
have been, to think as you have
been, and to believe as you have
been, then nothing in your
experience will change.

AUGUST 17

Why you want something
defines the essence of the *what* you
want, and the Universe always delivers to you the vibrational essence of your
desire. . . . So, when you think about *why* you
want something, you usually soften resistance;
but when you think about *when* it will come
to you or *how* it will come or *who* will help it
to come, you often add resistance, especially if you do not already know the
answers to those questions.

MAY 17

It is not possible
to stand still, or be stuck,
because Energy, and therefore,
life, is always in motion. Things are
always changing. But the reason it may
feel to you as if you are stuck is because
while you are continuing to think the same
thoughts, things *are* changing—but they
are changing to the same thing, over and
over. If you want things to change to different things, you must think different
thoughts. And that simply requires
finding unfamiliar ways of
approaching familiar
subjects.

AUGUST 16

When you iden-
tify any of the four basic
subjects of your life: Body, Home,
Relationships, or Work, a focusing of
Energy occurs. When you make more specific statements of desire, you activate the
Energy around those subjects even more. And
when you think about *why* you want those
things, you can usually be softening your resistance around the subject while adding even
more clarity and power to the thoughts.
Why you want something defines the
essence of the *what* you want. . . .
The Universe always delivers to you
the vibrational essence of
your desire.

Others cannot understand the vibrational content of your desires, and they cannot understand the vibrational content of where you are, so they are not in any way equipped to guide you. Even when they have the very best of intentions and want your absolute Well-Being, they do not know. And even though many of them attempt to be unselfish, it is never possible for them to separate their desire for you from their own desire for themselves.

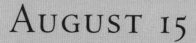

Once you begin the *Creation Box Process*, you will just be knocked over by the effectiveness and efficiency of the enormous Non-Physical staff who responds to your vibrational requests. When you ask, it is given; and as you play with the *Creation Box Process*, you will learn to let it in.

MAY 19

When you
remember that everyone
who asks is given, then how
wonderful and appropriate it is for
you to make the choices for *you*—
for the Universe operates much more
efficiently without a middleman inter-
ceding on your behalf. No one else
knows what is appropriate for you—
but you do. You always know,
in the moment, what is
best for you.

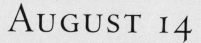

AUGUST 14

Most people offer
most of their vibrational
offerings in response to what
they are observing, but there is no
creative control in that. Your creative control comes only in *deliberately* offering thought—and when
you are visualizing, you have
complete control.

MAY 20

When you know that
you want something and you
notice that you do not have it, you
assume that there is something outside of yourself that is keeping it from
you, but that is never true. The only
thing that ever prevents your receiving something that you desire is that
your habit of thought is different
from your desire.

AUGUST 13

If you have not been
practicing thoughts of resistance,
the *Creation Box Process* will be all
that you will ever need to create
a wonderful life: You ask; Source
answers; you let it in. *You ask
and it is given.*

You were taught
to face reality before you
knew you were *creating* reality.
Do not face reality unless it is a reality you want to create—for any "reality"
only exists because someone has focused
it into being. . . . All those statistics that
are gathered about your own experiences
and about others are only about how
somebody has already flowed
Energy—they are not about any
hard-and-fast *now* reality.

AUGUST 12

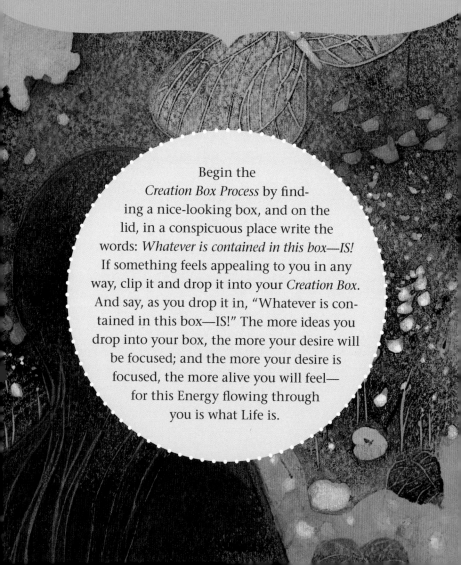

Begin the
Creation Box Process by finding a nice-looking box, and on the
lid, in a conspicuous place write the
words: *Whatever is contained in this box—IS!*
If something feels appealing to you in any
way, clip it and drop it into your *Creation Box*.
And say, as you drop it in, "Whatever is contained in this box—IS!" The more ideas you
drop into your box, the more your desire will
be focused; and the more your desire is
focused, the more alive you will feel—
for this Energy flowing through
you is what Life is.

Even the smallest
among you, your babies,
are offering vibrations that the
Universe is matching. And, like you,
your little ones are influenced by the
vibrations of those who surround them—
but, nevertheless, they are creating their
own reality. Like you, they did not begin
the creation of their life in this body
once they were in it. Long before their
physical birth, they set into motion
this life experience that they
are now living.

AUGUST 11

Life is not about tomorrow,
it is about right now. Life is
about how you are currently
molding the Energy!

If you were driving your vehicle at 100 miles per hour and you hit a tree, you would experience a very big crash. However, if you were to hit the same tree while your vehicle was traveling at just 5 miles per hour, the outcome would be considerably different. See the speed of your vehicle like the power of your desire. In other words, the more you want something, or the longer you have been focusing upon your desire, the faster the Energy moves. The tree in our analogy represents the resistance, or the contradictory thoughts, that may be present.

AUGUST 10

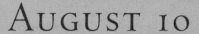

As you move through your day and as you become aware of something that you do *not* want, your desire about what you *do* want comes into clearer focus. And now, when you have been practicing a *Rampage of Appreciation,* you can easily refocus your awareness of what you do not want into your awareness of what you do want. Now you are the hands-on creator that you have come forth to be.

Your desire is
the natural result of the
contrast on which you are
focused. The entire Universe exists
to inspire the next new desire. And
so, if you are trying to avoid your own
desire, you are attempting to move
contrary to Universal Forces. . . .
Nothing in all of the Universe is
more natural than *your*
continuing desire.

AUGUST 9

You have to come to
remember that it makes no
difference whatsoever how any-
body is flowing back at you, otherwise
you are going to be defensive—and you
cannot be *defensive* and *appreciative* at the
same time. When you concentrate on *appreciating*, then *appreciation* comes right
back—but you are really not looking
for appreciation to come to you; you
want the *feeling* of appreciation
flowing *through* you.

MAY 25

There is no
desire that anyone holds
for any other reason than that
they believe they will feel better in
the achievement of it. Whether it is a
material object, a physical state of being,
a relationship, a condition, or a circum-
stance—at the heart of every desire is the
desire to feel good. And so, the standard
of success in life is not the things or
the money—the standard of success
is absolutely the amount of
joy you feel.

AUGUST 8

We want you to feel
the value of connecting with
Non-Physical Energy—and
appreciation is the easiest and fastest
way. When your desire to connect
with the Non-Physical Energy is
sufficient, you will find dozens of
ways, in every hour, to make
your *appreciation* flow.

Appreciation and self-love are the most important aspects you could ever nurture. *Appreciation of others and the appreciation of yourself are the closest vibrational matches to Source Energy of anything we have ever witnessed anywhere in this Universe.*

AUGUST 7

Once you have
made a decision that
nothing is more important than
that you feel good, and you have
decided that you are going to consciously look for some things to appreciate today, the object of your attention
has now become the feeling of appreciation. You have now established a circuit
between you and that object of appreciation that the *Law of Attraction* will
begin working on immediately—
so, you will start seeing more
things to appreciate
right away.

MAY 27

If you criticize
someone or even find
fault with yourself, your result-
ing feeling would not feel good,
because this thought of criticism is
so very different from that of your
Source. In other words, because you
have chosen a thought that does not
match who-you-really-are, you can,
in this moment, through your
emotions, feel the discord
of your choice.

Whenever you are
looking for things to
appreciate, you have control of
your own vibrational offering and your
own point of attraction; but when you are
responding to the way others seem to feel
about you, you have no control. . . . You do
not know what happened to them today, and
you do not how they are living, so you cannot understand why they react to you in the
way they do—and you cannot control it.
However, when you are more interested
in how *you* feel than how they feel
about you, you do have control
of your experience.

We do teach *selfishness,* for if you are not selfish enough to deliberately align with the Energy of your Source, you have nothing to give anyway. Some worry, "If I selfishly achieve what I want, wouldn't I be unfairly taking it from others?" But that concern is based on the misconception that there is a limit of available abundance. They worry that if they take too much of the pie, others will be left with nothing, while, in reality . . . *the pie expands in proportion to the vibrational requests of all of you.*

AUGUST 5

You may blame yourself
for not being strong enough
to *appreciate* some unhappy people
in spite of their negative emotional
offerings toward you. Well, we would
never suggest that you be able to look at
something you do not want and feel good
about it. Instead, look for things that
cause you to feel *appreciation* when you
find them—and then the *Law of
Attraction* will bring you more
things like those.

MAY 29

There are some who fear
that a selfish person may
deliberately intend harm to
another, but it is not possible for
someone who is connected to
Source Energy to wish harm upon
another—for those vibrations
are not compatible.

A desire to
appreciate is a very good
first step; and then as you find
more things that you would like to
feel appreciation for, it quickly gains
momentum. And as you want to feel
appreciation, you *attract* something
to *appreciate*. And as you *appreciate* it,
then you attract something else to
appreciate, until, in time, you are
experiencing a *Rampage of
Appreciation.*

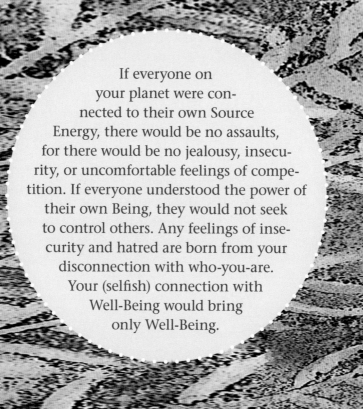

MAY 30

If everyone on
your planet were con-
nected to their own Source
Energy, there would be no assaults,
for there would be no jealousy, insecurity, or uncomfortable feelings of competition. If everyone understood the power of
their own Being, they would not seek
to control others. Any feelings of insecurity and hatred are born from your
disconnection with who-you-are.
Your (selfish) connection with
Well-Being would bring
only Well-Being.

We are often
asked, *Isn't <u>love</u> a better
word than <u>appreciation?</u>
Isn't <u>love</u> more descriptive of the
Non-Physical Energy?* And we say
that *love* and *appreciation* are really
the same vibration. Some use the
word *gratitude,* or a feeling of
thankfulness, for all of these
words are descriptive of
Well-Being.

It is not necessary for everyone else (or *anyone* else, for that matter) to understand what you are learning here in order for *you* to live a wonderful experience. Once you remember who-you-are, and once you deliberately reach for thoughts that hold you in vibrational alignment with who-you-are, *your* world will also fall into alignment—and Well-Being will show itself to you in all areas of your life experience.

Every time you *appreciate* something, every time you *praise* something, every time you *feel good* about something, you are telling the Universe: "More of this, please." You need never make another verbal statement of an intent—*and if you are mostly in a state of appreciation, all good things will flow to you.*

JUNE 1

When you
want something that
you do *not* believe is possible,
when you hold a desire for something that you do *not* expect—
although a strong enough desire
can override a weaker belief—it
does not unfold easily, for you are
not *allowing* it into your
current experience.

AUGUST 1

Once you
become oriented toward
looking for things to *appreciate*,
you will find that your day will be
filled with such things. Your thoughts
and feelings of *appreciation* will flow from
you naturally. And, often, while in the
midst of a genuine feeling of *appreciation*
for someone or something, you will feel
ripples of thrill bumps—those sensations are confirming your alignment with your Source.

JUNE 2

Unfortunately, many people think that the uncomfortable feeling of wanting something they do not expect to experience is what the feeling of *desire* is; they no longer recognize the feeling of pure desire as that fresh, eager feeling of expectancy that they knew when they were younger. The feeling of pure desire is always delicious, as it represents the vibrations that are stretched out before you, into your unseen future, preparing the way for the *Law of Attraction* to match things up on your behalf.

In the *Rampage of Appreciation Process,* you actually set your vibrational frequency to one of allowing what you have asked for into your experience. You have been asking, in every day of your experience, and Source has answered, without exception. And now, in your mode of *appreciation,* you are in the practice of receiving. You are now engaging in the last step in the process of *Creation* (you are letting it in).

JUNE 3

As we ask, *Why would you like to be over there?* often the reply is, "Because I'm not happy over here where I'm standing." We then explain that it is important to talk about what is believed to be "over there" and to try to find the *feeling-place* of what is "over there." For as long as someone is talking about, and *feeling,* what is "over here," it is not possible for them to get "over there."

In the wonderful feeling of the vibration of appreciation, where no resistance exists, you will be in an exaggerated state of *allowing;* you will be in the vibrational state where the things that you desire can flow easily into your experience. The better it gets, the better it gets!

JUNE 4

If you have been
accustomed to thinking
and speaking about where you
are currently standing, it is not an
easy thing to suddenly shift your vibrations and to now begin thinking and feeling something that is very different. In fact,
the *Law of Attraction* says that you do not
have access to thoughts and feelings that
are very far from where you have recently
been vibrating, but, with some effort,
you could find other better-feeling
thoughts that *are* within
your reach.

The more you
find something to *appreci-
ate,* the better it feels; the better
it feels, the more you want to do it;
the more you do it, the better it feels;
the better it feels . . . the more you want
to do it. The *Law of Attraction* assists with
the powerful momentum of these positive thoughts and feelings until—with
very little time and effort—you will
find your heart singing in your
joyous alignment with
who-you-really-are.

With a determination to feel better, you could change the subject and therefore find other thoughts with better-feeling vibrations—but vibrational shifting is usually a gradual process. In fact, a continual attempt, in defiance of the *Law of Attraction,* to try to jump vibrational ranges is a major factor in the feelings of discouragement that eventually cause people to conclude that they really do not have control of their own life experiences.

The more you
practice *appreciation,* the
less resistance you will have in
your own vibrational frequencies;
and the less resistance you have, the
better your life will be. Also, by practicing a *Rampage of Appreciation,* you will
become accustomed to the feeling of
higher vibrations, so that if you ever
revert to an old pattern of conversation
that causes resistance in your vibration, you will notice it early on,
before the vibration gets
too strong.

After focusing your attention on a subject for only a few seconds, the *Law of Attraction* begins to respond. Within 17 seconds of focusing on something, a matching vibration becomes activated. And now, when you repeatedly return to a pure thought, maintaining it for at least 68 seconds, in a short period of time (hours in some cases or a few days in others), that thought becomes a dominant thought. And once you achieve a dominant thought, you will experience matching manifestations until you change it.

Once it is your primary intention, as you move through your day, to find things to *appreciate*, you are practicing a vibration of less resistance, and you are making your connection to your own Source Energy stronger. Because the vibration of *appreciation* is the most powerful connection between the physical you and the Non-Physical You, this process will also put you in a position to receive even clearer guidance from your Inner Being.

JUNE 7

There
is no reason to
worry about your thoughts,
for they are not like a loaded gun
that may wreak powerful and instanta-
neous destruction. For although the *Law of
Attraction* is powerful, the basis of your experience is that of Well-Being. And even though
your thoughts are magnetic and expand with
your attention, you have plenty of time—
as soon as you become aware of any negative feelings—to begin to choose other
less-resistant thoughts and thereby choose a more desired
outcome.

JULY 26

The *Rampage of Appreciation Process* is not about finding something troubling and fixing it; this is a process of practicing the higher vibrations. The longer you focus upon things that feel good to you, the easier it is for you to maintain those vibrational frequencies that feel good. Make it your objective to choose objects of attention that easily evoke your *appreciation,* and the more you maintain those good-feeling frequencies, the more the *Law of Attraction* will deliver to you other thoughts, experiences, people, and things that match your practiced vibration.

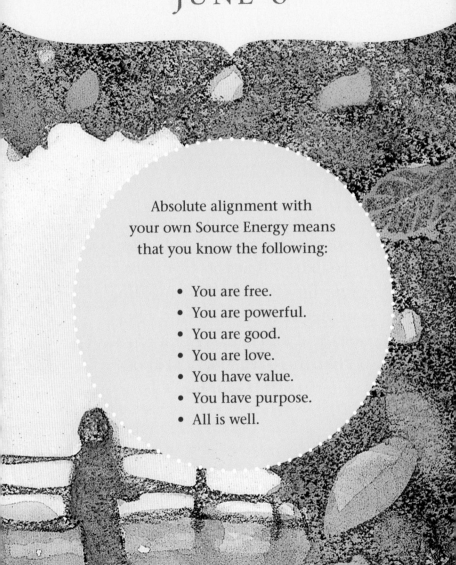

JUNE 8

Absolute alignment with
your own Source Energy means
that you know the following:

- You are free.
- You are powerful.
- You are good.
- You are love.
- You have value.
- You have purpose.
- All is well.

You are the creator of
your own experience whether
you know that you are or not.
Your life experience is unfolding
in precise response to the vibrations that radiate as a result of your
thoughts—whether you know
that it is or not.

JUNE 9

A scale of your
emotions would look
something like this:

1. Joy/Knowledge/
   Empowerment/
   Freedom/Love/
   Appreciation
2. Passion
3. Enthusiasm/
   Eagerness/
   Happiness
4. Positive
   Expectation/Belief
5. Optimism
6. Hopefulness
7. Contentment
8. Boredom
9. Pessimism
10. Frustration/Irrita-
    tion/Impatience
11. "Overwhelment"
12. Disappointment
13. Doubt
14. Worry
15. Blame
16. Discouragement
17. Anger
18. Revenge
19. Hatred/Rage
20. Jealousy
21. Insecurity/Guilt/
    Unworthiness
22. Fear/Grief/
    Depression/Despair/
    Powerlessness

It does not matter
how good you feel or how
fast you feel it—the only thing
that matters is that you *consciously*
discover some relief, no matter how slight
it is, and that you understand that your
relief has come in response to some *deliberate*
effort that you have offered. For when you
are able to consciously find relief, then you
have regained creative control of your
own experience, and then you are
on your way to wherever you
wish to go.

Word labels for
your emotions are not
absolutely accurate for every
person who feels the emotion. In
fact, giving word labels to the emotions could cause confusion and dis-
tract you from the real purpose of your
Emotional Guidance Scale. The thing
that matters most is that you consciously reach for a feeling that is
improved. The word for the
feeling is not important.

Through observing, remembering, pondering, and discussing, you have practiced thoughts that have become more powerful thoughts or beliefs, which now dominate your point of attraction. And each thought you consider, or focus upon, causes you to feel an emotional response. And so, over time, you have come to feel certain ways about certain things. We call that your *Emotional Set-Point.*

JUNE 11

There are so many who have convinced you that your *anger* is inappropriate—but, of course, they cannot feel the improvement that the *angry* thought really is. But when you *consciously* know that you have *chosen* an *angry* thought that has brought you relief, then you can consciously know that you can move from the *angry* thought to a less resistant one, such as *frustration*, and then up the *Emotional Guidance Scale* you go—right back into your full alignment.

JULY 22

There are times
when friends can prod or
tease you into a better-feeling
thought, but at other times their
prodding or teasing just makes you feel
worse. Any success they may have had in
helping you feel better has been, for the
most part, about how far out of alignment
you already were, because while it is easy
to make small vibrational jumps, it is
difficult, or even impossible, to
make large ones.

JUNE 12

There is tremen-
dous value when you are
able to *deliberately* cause even the
slightest improvement in the way you
feel, for even in that small emotional
improvement, you may have regained a
measure of control. And even though you
may not have fully exercised your control,
you no longer feel powerless. And so,
your trek back up the *Emotional Guidance Scale* is now not only possible,
but it is relatively easy.

JULY 21

Remember that the *Law of Attraction* is a powerful *Law,* and that it is not possible for you to find and hold a thought if your current *vibrational set-point* is very different from that thought. *You only have access to thoughts whose vibrations are somewhere in your current vibrational range.*

Someone outside of you does not know if your chosen thought of anger is an improvement for you; only you know—by the relief that you feel—the appropriateness of any thought. Until you decide that you are going to guide yourself by the way you feel, you can make no steady progress toward your own desires.

Unconditional love is really about wanting so much to remain in connection with your Source of love that you deliberately choose thoughts that allow your connection (no matter what manifestations may be happening nearby). And when you are able to control your point of attraction by deliberately choosing better-feeling thoughts, the conditions that surround you have to change. The *Law of Attraction* says that they must.

A key to regain-
ing your wonderful feeling
of personal empowerment and
control is to decide, right now, no
matter how good or how bad you are
feeling, that you are going to do your best
to make the best of it. Reach for the best-
feeling thought that you have access to
right now; and as you do that again and
again, in a short period of time you
will find yourself in a very good-
feeling place. That is just the
way it works!

Deliberate Creation is not about the condition changing and then your finding a better feeling in response to the changed condition. *Deliberate Creation* is about choosing a thought that feels good when you choose it—which then causes the condition to change.

JUNE 15

Desire, for many people,
often feels like yearning, for while
they are focused upon something that
they want to experience or have, they are
equally aware of its absence. And so, while
they are using *words of desire*, they are offering
a *vibration of lack*. They come to think that the
feeling of desire is like wanting something that
they do not have. But there is no feeling of
lack in pure desire. . . . *If you will keep
in mind that whenever you ask, it is always
given, then each of your desires will
now be pure, unresisted desire.*

JULY 18

You have no creative
power within the lives of
others, for they are offering their
own vibrations, which equal *their*
own point of attraction, just as you
are offering your own vibrations,
which equal *your* own point
of attraction.

JUNE 16

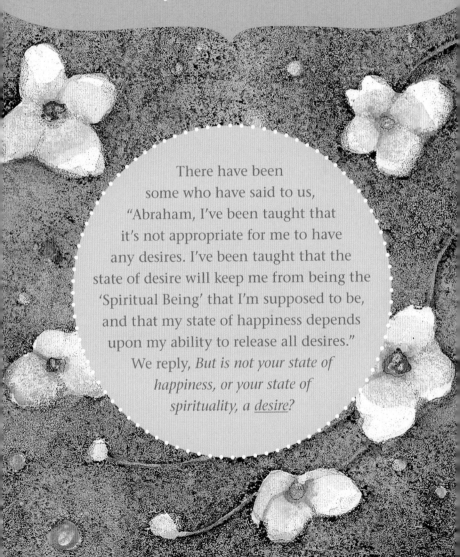

There have been
some who have said to us,
"Abraham, I've been taught that
it's not appropriate for me to have
any desires. I've been taught that the
state of desire will keep me from being the
'Spiritual Being' that I'm supposed to be,
and that my state of happiness depends
upon my ability to release all desires."
We reply, *But is not your state of
happiness, or your state of
spirituality, a <u>desire</u>?*

JULY 17

Without making the correlation between your thoughts and
feelings and the manifestations
that are occurring, you have no
conscious control of what happens
in your experience.

JUNE 17

When your desire feels so
big that it feels unreachable, it is
not on the verge of manifestation.
When your desire feels to you like it
is the next logical step—then it is
on the verge of manifestation.

JULY 16

The most satis-
fying aspect of *Deliberate
Creation* comes from being sensitive to the way the thoughts you
are thinking feel, for then it is possible
to modify a bad-feeling thought to one
that feels better, and to thereby improve
your point of attraction before something
unwanted manifests. *It is far easier—before
an unwanted physical manifestation
appears—to deliberately change the
direction of your thought to something that feels better.*

JUNE 18

You can tell by
the way you *feel* whether
your vibration is in the place
where you are allowing Universal
Forces to deliver your desire to you
now—or not. With practice, you will
know whether you are on the brink of
a manifestation or whether it is still
in the becoming stages; but, most
important, *once you are in control
of the way you feel, you will
enjoy it all. . . .*

There are two surefire ways to understand what your vibrational offering is: Notice what is happening in your experience (for what you are focused upon and what is manifesting are always a vibrational match), and notice how you feel (because your emotions are giving you constant feedback about your vibrational offering and your point of attraction).

*Once you are
in control of the way you
feel, you will enjoy it all:* You
will enjoy your exposure to the
variety and contrast that helps you
identify your desire—and you will
enjoy the sensation of your own
desire that is being launched from
your own valuable perspective
and is flowing from you.

JULY 14

When
you remember an
incident from a past experience, you are focusing Energy.
When you are imagining something
that may occur in your future, you are
also focusing Energy. And, of course, when
you are observing something in your *now*,
you are focusing Energy. It makes no difference whether you are focusing on the past,
present, or future . . . you are still focusing Energy—and your point of attention, or focus, is causing you to
offer a *vibration* that is your
point of attraction.

JUNE 20

*Once you are in control
of the way you feel, you will
enjoy it all:* You will enjoy the sensation of your conscious awareness when you are not a vibrational match to your own desire—and you will enjoy the sensation of deliberately bringing yourself back into vibrational alignment with your desire.

JULY 13

Just as you would
not deaden your fingertips to
desensitize them to heat, or cover
your fuel-gauge indicator on your
vehicle with a "Happy Face" sticker
because you do not like seeing that you are
out of fuel, you would not want to mask your
own feelings, pretending to feel different from
how you really feel. For pretending in this way
does nothing to change your vibrational point
of attraction. The only way you can do so is
to change your vibrational offering, and
when you do change your vibrational offering, the way you feel
changes, too.

Once you are in control of the way you feel, you will enjoy it all: You will feel relief as doubts slip away and as the secure feelings of Well-Being replace them.

These teachings have been designed for the powerful reason of helping you realign with the Energy that is really You. And in that process, you will return to your natural joy. Oh, and, yes, there will be the added side benefit of helping you achieve anything you have ever desired.

JUNE 22

Once you are in control of the way you feel, you will enjoy it all: You will enjoy sensing things that are about to happen, you will enjoy seeing things beginning to fall into place, and you will adore witnessing the manifestations of your desires.

JULY 11

It is our absolute
promise to you that your
life will improve with the
application of these teachings, for
you cannot apply them without improving the way you feel. And you cannot
improve the way you feel without releasing
resistance and thereby improving your point
of attraction. And when you improve your
point of attraction, the *Law of Attraction*
must bring you circumstances, events,
relationships, experiences, sensations, and powerful evidence of
your shift in vibration.
It is *Law!*

JUNE 23

*Once you are in control
of the way you feel, you will
enjoy it all:* You will revel in the
conscious awareness that you have
deliberately molded your desires into
being in as real a way as if you had
created a statue with the clay in
your own hands.

Those who observe you
will be amazed by the things
they begin to see happening in your
experience and by the joy that you
will obviously be radiating. And you will
explain, with the confidence and cer-
tainty that you were born with, "I have
found a way to allow the Well-Being
flow that is natural to me. I have
learned to practice the
Art of Allowing."

JUNE 24

Once you are in control of the way you feel, you will enjoy it all: You will adore the sensations you feel as you align, again and again, with the fruits of your own experience.

JULY 9

The processes presented in these
Teachings of Abraham are designed
to help you remove the resistance
from your path, for there is nothing
more delicious than moving at the
speed of life that you are accustomed
to—with no trees in the way.

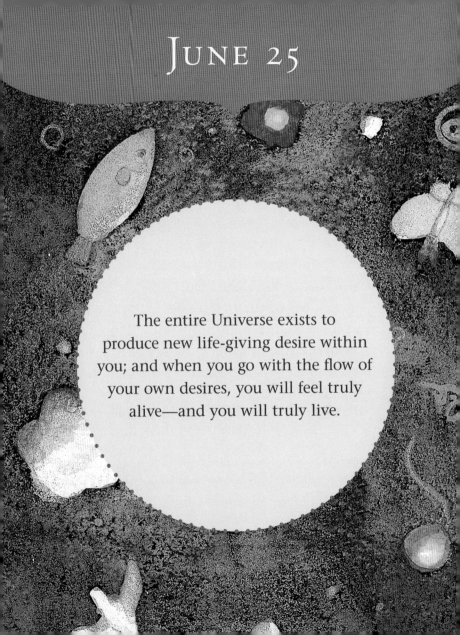

The entire Universe exists to produce new life-giving desire within you; and when you go with the flow of your own desires, you will feel truly alive—and you will truly live.

JULY 8

The most
important thing for you
to acknowledge before you
apply any of these processes is how
you are feeling right now—and how
you would like to feel. At the beginning
of each process, we indicate an emotional
range that we suggest for each one. Any
of the processes that fall within the
emotional range that you believe
you are feeling right now is a
perfect place to begin.

Now that you have made it this far into these teachings, you have been reminded of many things that you have always known: You now remember that you are an extension of Source Energy and that you have come into your physical body, into this Leading-Edge time-space reality, for the purpose of joyously taking thought beyond that which it has been before.

JULY 7

In the same way
that you did not develop
your resistant patterns all at
once, you will not release them all
at once—but you *will* release them.
Process by process, game by game (we
use the word *game* interchangeably
with *process*), and day by day, you will
gradually but steadily return to
being a person who allows your
own natural Well-Being to
flow to you.

JUNE 27

You now remember that you have an *Emotional Guidance System* within you that helps you to know, in every moment, how much of your connection to your Source you are allowing right now.

JULY 6

Your habit of
resistant thought is the
only thing that ever keeps you
from *allowing* the things you desire.
And although you certainly did not
intentionally develop these resistant patterns of thought, you did pick them up
along your physical trail, bit by bit, and
experience by experience. But one thing
is very clear: *If you do not do something
that causes a different vibrational
offering, then nothing in your
experience can change.*

JUNE 28

You now remember that the
better you feel, the more you are
in alignment with who-you-really-
are; and the worse you feel, the
more you are disallowing that
important connection.

JULY 5

If there is something
about your life that you wish
to improve—perhaps something
missing that you would like to
include, or something unwanted
that you would like to release—
these Teachings of Abraham will
be of immense value to you.

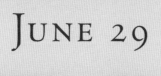

JUNE 29

You now remember that there is nothing that you cannot be, do, or have; and you remember that if your dominant intention is to feel good— and that if you try to make the best of where you are—you must reach your natural state of joy.

JULY 4

There is no Source of "evil" or Source of sickness or lack. *You may allow or you may resist Well-Being— but everything that happens to you is all your own doing.*

JUNE 30

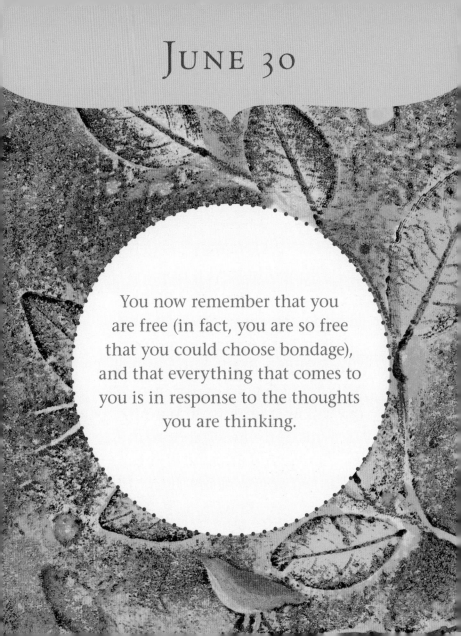

You now remember that you
are free (in fact, you are so free
that you could choose bondage),
and that everything that comes to
you is in response to the thoughts
you are thinking.

JULY 3

And, most
important, you now
remember that Well-Being
is the basis of your world, and
that unless you are doing something that is disallowing it, then
Well-Being is your experience. You
may allow it or resist it, but only a
Stream of wellness, abundance,
clarity, and all good things
that you desire . . .
flows.

You now remember that whether you are thinking about your past, present, or future, you are offering a vibration that equals your point of attraction.

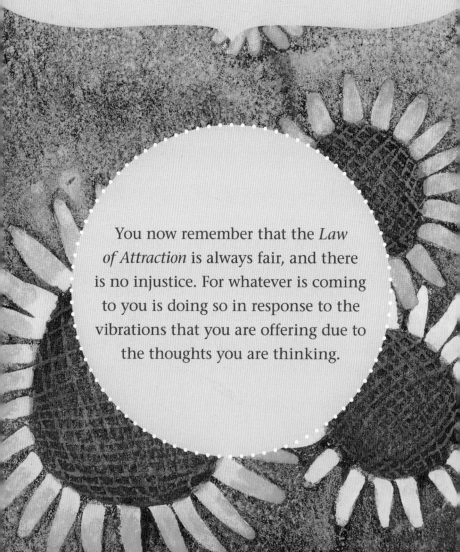

JULY 2

You now remember that the *Law of Attraction* is always fair, and there is no injustice. For whatever is coming to you is doing so in response to the vibrations that you are offering due to the thoughts you are thinking.